Presented to

_____

by

_____

on

_____

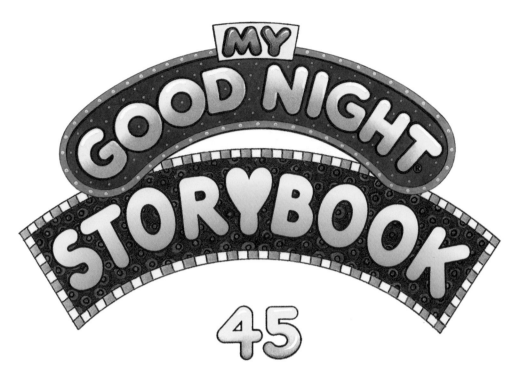

# 45

## Devotional Stories
## for Little Ones

written by Susan L. Lingo
illustrated by Kathy Parks

Standard
PUBLISHING
*Bringing The Word to Life*™

Cincinnati, Ohio

*My Good Night® Storybook* is a revised edition of *My Good Night® Devotions*.

Scriptures quoted from the *International Children's Bible® New Century Version®*. Copyright ©
1986, 1988, 1999 by Tommy Nelson™, a division of Thomas Nelson, Inc., Nashville, Tennessee
37214. Used by permission.

11  10  09  08  07  06  05          9 8 7 6 5 4 3 2 1

Library of Congress Cataloging-in-Publication Data

Lingo, Susan L.
My good night storybook : 45 devotional stories for little ones /
written by Susan L. Lingo ; illustrated by Kathy Parks.-- Rev. ed.
     p. cm.
     Rev. ed. of: My good night devotions. c2000.
     Includes bibliographical references and indexes.
     ISBN 0-7847-1542-4 (hardcover : alk. paper)
     1. Christian children--Prayer-books and devotions--English.
     2. Bedtime prayers  I. Lingo, Susan L. My good night devotions. II. Title.

BV4870.L54 2005
242'.62--dc22                                        2004017878

## from Susan

*If we placed all our playmates end to end,*
*we'd still find that Jesus is our best friend!*
*Jesus said, "I call you friends" (John 15:15).*


## from Kathy

*With love to all God's good thinkers,*
*who listen for his guidance every day.*

# Contents

# Dear Parents and Caregivers,

The lives of children (and grown-ups!) are busy, busy, busy! There are so many places to go, people to know, and ways to grow. Sometimes it's hard to find the time to do even the simplest things. *My Good Night® Storybook* will help you and your child find some quiet time to be together—and get to know God even better!

If you've read *My Good Night® Bible,* you've already met our favorite firefly friend, Night-Light. Now snuggle up as Night-Light introduces us to his friends and their families. Delightful stories about these charming kid characters and their everyday joys and troubles will help your child discover the way God's Word works—all the time! Reading *My Good Night® Storybook* together will bless your child's active, developing mind with sweet, sound messages of God's love and wisdom.

## Welcome to the neighborhood!

Hi! I'm Night-Light. Let's take a walk together down Apple Tree Lane and meet all of our friends! You'll learn more about each of these friends as you read their stories. And you'll learn more about God!

Sophie and Sam Springly are brother and sister. Sophie is five and her brother is just a year older. Sophie is full of spunk and likes to do things by herself. Sam enjoys teasing his little sister. They argue sometimes, but they both love spaghetti, swing sets, and their little patch-eyed pup, Poochie.

Max and Polly Popple live next door to the Springlys'. Polly is an almost-three-year-old bundle of wiggly, giggly joy. Polly's brother, Max, is five and loves to play with his best friend, Sophie.

Mia Chang lives in the pretty white house across the street from Sophie and Sam. Mia loves her fluffy kitten, Stormy, her pet parrot, Kei-Kei, and her new baby brother, Joe. Mia is four and is eager to know everything she can know, especially how to read.

Seven-year-old **Jimmy Lopez** is the big kid on the block and lives with his mom in the blue house at the end of Apple Tree Lane. Jimmy has a big backyard with rows of apple trees and a shed for his friendly pony, Schnickelfritz.

**Mr. Morisky's** store on the corner is a favorite place of all the kids. Sweet ice cream, inviting toys, and fresh fruits and vegetables fill Mr. Morisky's shelves while bushels of love fill his heart. He's always ready to listen to anyone and often offers some very good free advice.

Welcome to the neighborhood! All of our friends are so glad to meet you! We hope you enjoy your time on Apple Tree Lane.

# How to use this book

Use *My Good Night® Storybook* alone or combine it with
*My Good Night® Bible* or *My Good Night® Prayers* to create a
peaceful, calming bedtime routine. The stories in this book are
designed to coordinate with the stories in *My Good Night® Bible*
and the quiet times in *My Good Night® Prayers*—they even use
the same Bible verses! For example, the story on page 21 of this
book can be paired with the Bible story on page 21 of *My Good
Night® Bible* and the quiet time prayer and song on page 21 in
*My Good Night® Prayers.* The repetition of simple themes and
verses makes it even easier for your child to enjoy, understand,
and remember God's Word.

1. *Begin with the Story Time Rhyme (page 16).* After toys are
picked up, teeth are brushed, and pajamas are on, sing or say
the rhyme to signal that story time is beginning.

2. *Choose a story and read the "God said" or "Jesus said"
Scripture verse together.* Each Bible verse presents the theme for
that story, such as "Obey me" or "Forgive other people." These
are simple verses that children can actually learn and put to
use in their lives!

3. *Read the story to your child.* Each story has been thoughtfully
written for young children. Short sentences, simple words,
alliteration, rhyme, and rhythm all help capture children's
attention. The lively devotional stories are memorable illustrations of the biblical themes, giving children solid examples for
seeking God and obeying Jesus in familiar situations.

4. *Look at the pictures. My Good Night® Storybook* is filled with lovingly designed illustrations that help bring the characters to life. "Find and point" picture activities located at the bottom of the story pages help focus children's attention.

5. *Read the devotional thoughts.* Our firefly friend, Night-Light, draws children even closer to the message with his comments on the related Bible story. His thoughts will also help children relate the message to their lives.

6. *Talk to God together.* Use the prayer provided or pray in your own words. Let your child say a prayer of her own, too.

7. *Sing the Slumber Song (page 17).* Leave your child with the sound of your voice and the reminder of God's love.

## Together-time tips for bedtime or anytime

Use these helpful hints and terrific tips to make learning about God more powerful and your together times more enjoyable.

- Take your time. Slow down and set aside the worries of the day. Observe how many minutes it takes your child to get ready for quiet time. Be sure to allow enough "settling down" time—for both of you!

- Involve your child and encourage God-centered problem-solving. When a character has a problem or a decision to make, stop and ask your child what Jesus would do.

- If you use both *My Good Night® Bible* and *My Good Night® Storybook*, consider reading one story for bedtime and the accompanying story for nap time or for the next night. Invite your child to retell the previous story before reading the matching one. Be sure to read the Bible verses. You may also want to use the prayers, songs, and rhymes from *My Good Night® Prayers* to support the stories you read.

- Play quiet word games. Go to pages 112 and 113. Let your child point to the characters and say their names. Choose a character's name and identify the beginning sound. Have your child look through the other pictures in the book or in the room for items that begin with that same sound.

- Match stories with real situations. If your child needs to forgive, read a story that deals with forgiveness. Look for ways to reinforce devotion themes with life's everyday experiences. Continually remind your child of God's love.

- Share the warmth of the children on Apple Tree Lane as they learn about God's love and obeying Jesus. Enjoy these special stories at bedtime, nap time, "cool-down" time—anytime you and your child want to experience the joy of God's truth and love.

God bless you and sleep tight!

*Susan Lingo*

# Story Time Rhyme

*(to the tune of "The Mulberry Bush")*

Let's join the kids
in the neighborhood
and learn why God
is great and good.
We'll meet new friends and
share our love,
and learn of God above!

# Slumber Song

*(to the tune of "Jesus Loves Me")*

Let's tuck you in, turn off the light—
now it's time to say "Good night."
God is watching over you,
he keeps us safe the whole night through.

Chorus:
God's love is near us,
God's love is near us,
God's love is near us,
sleep tight, I love you, dear.

I go to bed
and sleep in peace.
Lord, only you keep me safe.

Psalm 4:8

Hi! It's me, Night-Light, your firefly friend! I can't wait to learn about God with my friends. What fun! And if you look closely, you'll see me in one of the pictures of every story you read. Let's start reading together now!

# The Secret Ingredient

*God said, "I made the earth." Isaiah 45:12*

Sophie Springly liked to make things. She colored a get-well card for Grandpa. She painted a rainbow for Daddy. And today, Sophie was making flowers for Mommy's birthday! She gathered pretty tissue paper, tape, and drinking straws.

Then Sophie called her best friend, Max Popple. "C'mon over! We'll make flowers!" Sophie said. Max said, "Only God makes flowers." But he came over anyway.

"We can make flowers by twisting tissue paper," said Sophie. "Only God makes flowers," repeated Max. But he took a piece of bright yellow tissue paper anyway. Sophie twisted her pink paper this way and that, but her flower looked like a floppy old hat. Max twisted his paper that way and this, but his flower looked like a wrinkly old fish!

"Only God makes flowers," reminded Max. "But your flower is kind of pretty."

"I wanted to give Mommy the most beautiful flower in the world!" said Sophie sadly. "How does God make such beautiful flowers? He must have a secret ingredient!"

*Count the straws.*

Max and Sophie thought hard. They thought about pretty little flowers. They thought about beautiful big mountains. And they thought about cute baby birds. Suddenly Max smiled and shouted, "I know! It's not just the flower or mountain or bird—it's the love that God added when he made the world! *That's* what makes everything he made soooo beautiful."

"That's the secret ingredient!" shouted Sophie. "Now I know what to do! I'll give Mommy my flowers and lots of love, too!"

*Who is Sophie kissing?*
*What did Sophie and Max decide is God's secret ingredient?*

# A Bible Story to Remember

### Genesis 1:1–2:3

Who made the world? God made the
world! He made flowers and trees,
mountains and bees, birds, people, and
fish in the seas! And God made them all
with his own special ingredient—love!
Think about God's love for you. When
do you feel his love?

# A Prayer to Pray

*Dear God,*
*You're our Creator*
*in heaven above—*
*help us care for the world*
*with your special love.*
*Amen.*

# A Sleepy Time Activity

Let's make some pretty pretend
flowers! Scrunch tissue paper into
a flower shape and tape it to a
drinking straw. Hold your flower and
name some of your favorite things
God made. Look at your flower as
you fall asleep. Sleep tight!

# Name Game

*God said, "I have called you by name." Isaiah 43:1*

Mia Chang had a new kitten. It had long black fur. It had big yellow eyes. And it had the fluffiest tail Mia had ever seen! But the kitten didn't have a name.

"Why don't you call him 'Fluffy'?" said Sophie Springly. But Max Popple didn't like that. "Aww, that's a sissy name!" said Max. "How about calling him 'Max'?"

Mia laughed. "One Max is enough around here! I want a name that's just right." Just then, Jimmy Lopez rode up on his pony, Schnickelfritz. "Now there's a funny name!" laughed Max.

But Jimmy said, "Hey! 'Schnickelfritz' is a way to say 'little friend' in German. My grandpa told me that!"

Sophie sighed. "It's hard thinking up names. Do you think anyone knows all the names in the world?"

"God does," said Max. "God knows everyone's name because God made us. God even knows the name of your kitten before you do, Mia!"

*What animals do you see?*

"Well I wish God would just tell me my kitten's name," sighed Mia. Suddenly—BOOM! Crash! Boom!

"Wow, that was some loud thunder! Sounds like a big storm is coming!" said Max.

"And I think God just named my kitten," laughed Mia. "I'll call him 'Stormy'! Now let's go home, Stormy, before it rains cats and dogs!"

*Who's hiding from the thunder?*
*Who knows all the names in the world, including Stormy's?*

# A Bible Story to Remember

### Genesis 2:18-23; 3:20

The Bible tells us that God told Adam to give all the animals special names. We have special names, too. And God knows all of our names because he made us and he loves us. What's your name? Did you know God has an extra-special name for you? He calls you "his" because you belong to him!

# A Prayer to Pray

*I'm glad you call us
each by name.
You know and love us
all the same.
Amen.*

# A Sleepy Time Activity

Let's play a name game. See if you know these special names.
1. What's the name of our Creator?
2. What's the name of God's Son?
3. What's your best friend's name?
As you go to sleep, name some people who love you. Good night!

# Jimmy's Oh-My Pie

*God said, "Obey me." Jeremiah 7:23*

Seven-year-old Jimmy Lopez thought he was too old for directions. "I don't need directions. I can do everything by myself!" said Jimmy.

One day Jimmy read about how Noah obeyed God's directions for building the ark. "What did they eat on the ark?" Jimmy asked his mother.

"I'm sure God gave them directions for what foods to take," Mommy said as she rolled out a pie crust.

"Mmm," said Jimmy, "I bet they wanted pie! May I make a pie, too?"

"Of course!" said Mommy. "I'll show you how."

"I don't need directions," said Jimmy. "I've watched you make lots of pies. I can do it by myself!"

Jimmy mixed flour and salt and water in a bowl. "I won't add butter—it's too slimy!" said Jimmy. He mixed and rolled the dough. He put the dough in a pie pan and poured in the blueberry filling. Then Mommy popped the pie into the oven. "I don't need directions. See, I did it by myself!" smiled Jimmy proudly.

*How many spoons can you find?*

After dinner, Mommy admired Jimmy's beautiful pie—until she tried to cut it! She sawed and she chopped but—my-oh-my!—nothing could cut that blueberry pie!

Jimmy told Mommy what ingredients he put in the pie crust. Mommy laughed and said, "Oh my! You've baked a brick instead of a pie!"

"Brick, not pie? Guess I'll follow directions next time!" laughed Jimmy. "Too bad Noah didn't have this pie on the ark—it would've made a great anchor!"

*Name all the fruit you can find.*
*How did Jimmy find out that following directions is important?*

# A Bible Story to Remember

## Genesis 6:1–7:16

What a funny story! But following directions is no laughing matter, especially when it means obeying God! Noah loved God, so he obeyed God's directions to build the ark. Directions keep us safe and sound and happy every day. So be ready to follow God and shout, "I will obey!"

# A Prayer to Pray

*Dear God,*
*You give me directions*
*to show me the best way.*
*Please help me to follow you*
*day by day.*
*Amen.*

# A Sleepy Time Activity

Take turns giving and following directions such as, "Clap your hands and touch your nose." Then follow this direction: Think about how much God loves you and wants you to obey! Then close your eyes and go to sleep. Night-night!

# For Keeps!

*God said, "What God promises, he keeps." Numbers 23:19*

Sophie Springly was always making promises she didn't keep. She promised to give her brother, Sam, two cookies, but she ate them herself. She promised to give Mia Chang her old wagon. But Sophie kept it instead. Sophie never kept her promises to give things away because she wanted to keep everything she had!

Mrs. Bode's Sunday school class had a special project. The children wanted to collect a hundred books to give away. Everyone promised to bring books. "I'll bring my favorite book!" promised Sophie. But when she got home, Sophie looked at her favorite book and decided to keep it. I know I promised, she thought, but it won't matter.

Next Sunday, Mrs. Bode counted the books. "Ninety-seven, ninety-eight, ninety-nine. . . . We're one book short!" Mrs. Bode said. Sophie gulped. She knew she had broken her promise and it *did* matter! Sophie wanted to keep her book, but she wanted to keep her promise even more. What could she do?

*How many children do you see?*

"I'm sorry," Sophie said to her teacher. "I wanted to keep my promise, but I also wanted to keep my book."

Mrs. Bode smiled and said, "Sometimes promises are hard to keep, Sophie. But God also makes promises. God has promised to help you. And since God always keeps his promises, we can trust his promise to be true. So with God's help, you can make a promise and keep it, too!"

Sophie smiled. "I *can* do that! I can make my promises and keep them, too! And I promise to bring my book to you." And she did—the very next Sunday!

*What promise did Sophie keep?*
*Who helped Sophie keep her promise?*

# A Bible Story to Remember
### Genesis 7:6–8:12

When we make a promise, we need to keep it. That way, other people can trust us to do what we say. God always keeps his promises. He kept his promise to Noah, and he will keep his promises to us, too. We can trust God to do what he promises because he loves us.

# A Prayer to Pray

*Dear God,*
*You give me loving care.*
*You always hear my prayers.*
*Your promises are true,*
*so I will always count on you.*
*Amen.*

# A Sleepy Time Activity

God gave the world a sign of one of his promises—a rainbow in the sky! Can you name all the colors in a rainbow? As you go to sleep, think about a sky full of rainbows. Remember how beautiful and true God's promises are. Sleep tight!

# Tasty Thanks

*God said, "Show thanks to God." Psalm 50:14*

Max Popple had been playing all afternoon. He was hungry! "I think I could eat a jillion hamburgers now—or maybe a moose or even a house!" said Max, rubbing his empty tummy. Just then Dad said, "Dinner!"

Max raced through the door, washed his hands, and plopped down at the table. Everything looked so good! Aunt Martha said, "Yummy!" Polly said, "Mmmm!" Max's tummy said, "Grrrowl!" And Max shouted, "Let's eat!"

"First, let's thank God for our blessings," Daddy said. But Max said, "Awww, can't we pray *after* we eat today? A tummy that's full will have lots more to say!"

"Blessings sweeten everything!" Aunt Martha answered. "I'll go first! Thank you, God, for the people I see, and that I can be here with my family." Then Mommy prayed, "Father, I thank you for staying so near, and holding each one of us precious and dear."

"Me next! Me next!" said Polly, as she spilled some milk. Mommy mopped up the milk with a napkin, and Polly quietly said, "Thanks for na'kins, God. I love you!"

*How many plates do you see?*

Daddy said, "Dear Lord, I thank you for Max and our little Polly, and for making them healthy, lively, and jolly." Then it was Max's turn. He hoped God would hear his words and not his growling tummy! "Dear God, I love you so much 'cuz you treat us so good, and I 'specially give thanks for this wonderful food. Amen!"

As Max filled his plate and his tummy, he thought about how nice it was to thank God for his blessings. "This is a delicious dinner," said Aunt Martha. Max's mouth was full, but he gave a happy nod. Everything *does* taste better when we give thanks to God!

*What's Max eating?*
*What did Max do before he ate his dinner?*

# A Bible Story to Remember
### Genesis 8:13–9:17

After the flood, Noah took time with his family to give God thanks. It's great to have special times to get together and thank God. But we can thank God all day long! Giving thanks to God shows him how much we love and need him. And it helps us remember how good God is!

# A Prayer to Pray

*Dear God,*
*Please help me*
*remember to say*
*my thanks to you*
*every day.*
*Amen.*

# A Sleepy Time Activity

Night-Light wants to play a find-it game. See how many foods you can find in the story pictures. Then, as you go to sleep, thank God for as many things and people as you can think of. Good night!

# Not-So-Smarty Pants

*God said, "Remember that I am God." Isaiah 46:9*

Four-year-old Mia Chang thought she was very smart. She knew her letters and numbers and how to tie her shoes. Then Mia found an old dictionary on her daddy's bookshelf, and she thought she was even smarter! "Now I can know every word there is!" Mia told Sophie proudly. "I'll be the smartest person ever!"

"There's someone smarter," said Sophie, shaking her head. But Mia wouldn't listen. She took her special book everywhere. "I like being smart!" Mia told Sophie as they walked to Mr. Morisky's store for ice-cream cones.

"There's someone smarter," said Sophie, shaking her head. But Mia wouldn't listen. She was thinking of being smart—and of ice cream!

"Hello, girls!" smiled Mr. Morisky. "What flavor will it be today?" "Strawberry!" shouted Sophie. Mia proudly pointed to another flavor. "I'll have this one, Mr. Morisky! I'm smart and can read the name of every flavor you have!" Mr. Morisky looked a little surprised at Mia's choice, but he scooped up the ice cream for the girls.

*What colors are the candies?*

When Mia licked her ice cream, her nose wrinkled up. "Icky!" she exclaimed.

"You picked coffee ice cream!" said Sophie. Mia was disappointed. She sadly said, "I thought it was cocoa, not coffee! Guess I'm not very smart after all."

"You are smart, Mia," said Sophie, "But not just because you have a dictionary. God is the one who makes you able to be smart! He's smarter than anyone! God gave us our brains, and he teaches us through his words in the Bible. C'mon, I'll share my strawberry cone with you!"

*Why is Mia making a funny face?*
*Who is smarter than anyone?*

# A Bible Story to Remember

### Genesis 11:1-9

The Bible tells of some people who built a tall tower. They wanted to be smarter than God. But God tumbled that tower! No one is smarter than God above. He teaches us about mercy, forgiveness, and love. God gives us the Bible that's true, so we can grow smarter and obey him, too!

# A Prayer to Pray

*Dear God,*
*Please help me*
*remember what's true—*
*that no one is smarter*
*or wiser than you!*
*Amen.*

# A Sleepy Time Activity

Night-Light knows that learning God's Word helps us be wise. Repeat this verse from God as you go to sleep: "Remember that I am God" (Isaiah 46:9). Night-night!

# Just Trust

*God said, "They will trust in the Lord." Zephaniah 3:12*

Sam and Sophie Springly were brother and sister. Sam was six and Sophie was five but they both had turned-up noses, freckles, and shiny smiles. And like any brother and sister, they were sometimes the best of friends—and sometimes the worst!

Sam liked to play jokes on Sophie. Once, Sam set an alarm clock so that it would wake her up an hour too early for school. Another time, Sam put salt in the sugar bowl so Sophie's cereal tasted like pretzels! Sophie shouted, "Sam Springly, I can't trust you!" Sam just laughed.

The Springlys had a new piano. Sophie sat on the new piano stool and plinked the piano keys. "This stool is fun to spin!" giggled Sophie, as she twirled around and around. "Wheeee!" said Sophie, and she spun faster and faster and faster until WHUMP! The seat twirled right off and Sophie tumbled down.

"Oh, no!" said Sophie. "Spinning around was really such fun—"

"Wow, Sophie! Look what you've done!" said Sam, walking into the room.

*Who is smiling in the picture on the piano?*

"Sam! I knew I couldn't trust you. You made the stool fall apart!" yelled Sophie. "No, Sophie!" Sam said. "I didn't do it. But don't look so sad. I can fix it, I'm sure. It's not so bad." Sophie just frowned at her brother. But sure enough, Sam fixed the stool as good as new.

"See, Sophie, I told you," said Sam. "I like to play jokes on you because it's funny. But getting hurt and breaking things isn't funny. I wouldn't do that to you, or anybody! You *can* trust me about that."

Then Sophie smiled and said, "I'm sorry, Sam. I'm glad I have a brother like you. And I do trust you!"

*What is Sam fixing for Sophie?*
*Why didn't Sophie trust Sam at first?*

# A Bible Story to Remember

### Genesis 12:1-9; 15:5, 6

Sometimes people do things that make us not want to trust them. But we can always trust in God! God always knows what is best for us. Abraham and Sarah trusted God and God led them to a new home. Trusting God means being sure God will keep his promises, never leave us, and always love us!

# A Prayer to Pray

*Dear God,*
*I'm so glad*
*I can trust in you,*
*in all you say and*
*all you do.*
*Amen.*

# A Sleepy Time Activity

Night-Light says to close your eyes. No peeking! Now, do you think your room is still there? Of course it is! Now you can open your eyes. Even though we can't see God, we can trust that he is there, loving us all the time. Sleep tight!

# A Baby to Love

*God said, "What God promises, he keeps." Numbers 23:19*

The Changs had a new baby boy. But Mia wasn't happy. She was worried. "Maybe the baby will break all my toys. Maybe he'll cry a lot. Maybe Mommy and Daddy won't love me like before!"

"Mia, we promise we'll always love you. You're our best little girl and that's really true!" said Mommy and Daddy. But Mia was still worried.

Max and Polly Popple came to play. "Aren't you glad you have a baby brother?" asked Max while little Polly climbed into the sandbox. "No!" frowned Mia. "I think Mommy and Daddy aren't going to love me anymore."

"Sure they will," said Max. "My Mom and Dad love me *and* Polly. And it's fun to take care of babies—Polly, be careful!" said Max, as Polly toddled by the swings.

Mia was surprised and said, "*You* love Polly, too?" Max laughed. "Sure, well, mostly," he said with a smile. "I wasn't sure I liked her much when she chewed my crayons. But I forgave her. Now I think Polly's pretty cool!" Max gave Polly a big-brother squeeze as she tumbled into his lap.

*What is Stormy chasing?*

When Max and Polly left, Mia ran into her house.
Daddy gave Mia a hug. "We love you, Mia!" said Daddy.
"And we love your new brother, Joe. Want to hold him?"

Mia smiled. She knew that Mommy and Daddy loved
her—and now they loved Joe, too. Mia cuddled baby Joe
and whispered, "Joe, I promise I'll always love you. You're
my best baby brother and that's really true!"

*Which toys are Stormy's?*
*Who did Mia promise to love?*

# A Bible Story to Remember

### Genesis 18:1-15; 21:1-7

God showed his love for Abraham and
Sarah by keeping his promise to give
them a baby. God promises his love to
everyone: mother, father, sister, brother,
daughter, and son. And just as God
promises to love us each day, we can
love each other in so many ways!

# A Prayer to Pray

*Dear God,*
*I know you love me*
*and I love you, too.*
*Help me love my family*
*the way you want me to.*
*Amen.*

# A Sleepy Time Activity

Night-Light knows a way to say "I
love you." Point to your eye. Then
cross your arms in an X. Then point
at someone next to you. You just said
"I love you"! Say "I love you" to God
with these signs. God loves you, too!
Good night!

# Rescue Poochie

*God said, "I will save you." Jeremiah 30:10*

Sam Springly wanted a dog more than anything. All his friends had pets. And Sam was old enough for a dog, wasn't he? But Daddy said, "No dogs!" And Mommy said, "Dogs track in mud." Still, oh! how Sam longed for a dog of his own!

One morning, Sam saw a dog sitting under the shade tree. The puppy was skinny and small and had a funny spot over one eye. Mommy said, "Leave him alone. He'll go home." But after school the little pooch was still there!

"Please, Mommy," begged Sam and Sophie. "Can he come in? He's so skinny and hungry!"

"Just for a bite to eat," said Mommy. "But we won't keep him. We have no use for pooches here!" Sam and Sophie gave the little dog a nibble of ham and a drink of water. With all their hearts, they wanted to keep him.

"EEEEeeeek!" squealed Mommy. A tiny mouse skittered under the table. The little dog sprang into action. He yipped and yapped and yipped some more, till he chased that mousie out the door!

*Find three animals.*

"Oh, little pooch! You saved me from that awful mouse!" laughed Mommy. "Maybe we *could* use a brave watchdog around this house!"

"Yay!" shouted Sam. "Poochie saved you from the mouse and now we can save Poochie and give him a house!"

"And a home," smiled Mommy, as she patted brave little Poochie.

*Count the cookies.*
*Who saved Poochie when he needed help?*

# A Bible Story to Remember

### Exodus 2:1-10

The Bible tells us that when baby Moses needed help, God watched over him and kept him safe. God wants us to trust him, too, when we have trouble and don't know what to do. He is faithful and will always be there to help and heal and guide and care.

# A Prayer to Pray

*Dear God,*
*Thanks so much*
*for always being there*
*to help me and love me*
*and show that you care.*
*Amen.*

# A Sleepy Time Activity

Let's play a quiet game. Name some ways you can help your family, a friend, or a pet. Each time you name a way, point to your heart and say, "Thank you, God, for your help!" Think of how God saves you from trouble every day. Night-night.

# The Helpers Club

*God said, "You may serve me." Jeremiah 15:19*

The kids were bored—there was nothing to do. "It's
too hot to play," said Max Popple lazily. "Too hot," agreed
Sophie Springly. Mia Chang petted Stormy while little Polly
Popple tried to catch the kitten's swishing tail.

"Hi!" said Jimmy Lopez, riding up on Schnickelfritz.
"What's going on?" he asked. "Just a lot of nothing," said
Sam Springly. "Good!" said Jimmy, "You can help me
clean up Mr. Morisky's sidewalk. There are leaves and
papers all over after the storm last night. It will be fun!"

"Cleaning is fun?" asked Sophie. "Sure," said Jimmy.
"It's fun to help others. Hey! We could even form a helpers
club. Let's start right away!"

So the kids jumped up on that very hot day and
discovered that helping can be as fun as play. They swept
the sidewalk of the store, tossed out the papers, then did
more! They polished the windows and dusted shelves;
they did things for others instead of themselves.

*What is Mia holding?*

57

When they were finished, the store looked snappy.
And though they were hot, all the kids felt happy!

Mr. Morisky smiled, "Thanks for your help! Now how
about some ice cream for the Helpers Club?"

"Ice cream would be great!" said Jimmy, and all the
kids nodded their heads in happy agreement. Then Jimmy
said, "But the best part of serving is that when we serve
others, we also get to serve God!"

*Who's licking ice cream?*
*How did the Helpers Club serve God?*

# A Bible Story to Remember

### Exodus 3:1-15

God chose Moses to be his special helper. But anyone can serve others. There are many ways to help people. We can sweep, paint, clean, or even say kind words and pray! Serving others is what God wants us to do. And when we serve others with love, we serve God, too!

# A Prayer to Pray

*Dear God,*
*Please help me*
*look for ways*
*to serve others*
*all my days.*
*Amen.*

# A Sleepy Time Activity

Night-Light wants to draw pictures! Draw a picture of how you can serve God and others in some special way. As you go to sleep, hold your picture and thank God for the joy that serving brings. Sleep tight!

# Safe from the Storm

*God said, "I will save you." Jeremiah 30:10*

Crashhh! BOOM! What a rainstorm it was! But Max and Polly Popple were cozily playing in Max's room upstairs. Oh, they had made a marvelous mess! There were blocks and books all over the floor, an electric train, a flashlight, and more! Two-year-old Polly giggled as she and Max stacked up the blocks. Max was putting the last block on top when—CRASHHH-BOOOOM—everything went dark in Max's room!

"Waaaa!" wailed Polly. Max whispered, "Wow, it's dark!" Polly wailed even louder, "WaaAAA!"

Max knew Mommy and Daddy were downstairs, so he wasn't afraid. He didn't want Polly to be afraid either. Max wanted to help Polly. "Don't be afraid, Polly. It will be all right! See? Here's my flashlight. I'll flip on the light!" Max turned on his flashlight and Polly quit crying.

*What's on the top shelf?*

"Let's pretend we're crossing the Red Sea!"
said Max. They tiptoed around the building blocks
and scooted over the crayons and socks. Max and Polly
really had fun, and when Daddy appeared, all the lights
flickered on!

"I led Polly across the Red Sea and here to the
door as safe as can be!" shouted Max. Polly giggled and
clapped her hands. "Max helped!" shouted Polly.

Daddy smiled at their happy faces and at the sea of
toys scattered over the floor. "Now you and Polly can clean
up the sea and put it away as neat as can be!" he laughed.

*Find the train.*
*Why do you think Max wanted to help Polly?*

# A Bible Story to Remember

### Exodus 14

When Moses and the people came to the Red Sea, God helped them cross as safe as could be. God is with us and he'll help us, too. That's nice to know, isn't it? So if you're afraid, day or night, just call on God and you'll feel all right!

# A Prayer to Pray

*Dear God,*
*Thank you for*
*your saving care*
*and for promising me*
*you'll always be there.*
*Amen.*

# A Sleepy Time Activity

Night-Light wants to play a game to remind us how God keeps us safe. Tell how we can stay safe in these situations: at a swimming pool; crossing a street; in a crowded store. Think of how God keeps you safe all the time. Good night!

# An Answer for Sophie

*God said, "I will answer you." Jeremiah 33:3*

Sophie was having an unhappy day. She bumped her head on the dresser. She dribbled oatmeal down her new sweater. She even washed her hair with mouthwash instead of shampoo! Poor Sophie—what a day she was having!

"I need someone to talk to," said Sophie, "someone I can tell my troubles to!" Sophie saw Mommy writing on her rosebud paper. "Mommy—" began Sophie. But Mommy said, "Not now, Sophie dear. Later is better. Now I really must finish answering this letter."

Sophie walked into the family room. "Daddy—" she began. But Daddy whispered, "Not now, sweetie. Later we'll play ball. Right now I have to answer this telephone call!"

Poor Sophie! Didn't anyone have time to answer her? Would anyone listen to Sophie? Just then the doorbell rang. "I'll get it!" called Sophie, running to the door.

*How many plants do you see?*

65

Sophie opened the door and what did she see? A pretty balloon! "Oh, is it for me?" Sophie asked. Mia Chang's face popped out from behind the balloon. She handed Sophie the big pink balloon. "I had two balloons and wanted to share one with you!" smiled Mia.

Sophie smiled and giggled. She knew that someone had listened to her and sent Mia to cheer her up! Sophie smiled and thought, "Daddy answered the phone and Mommy her letter—but God answered me, and now I feel better!"

*What circle shapes can you find?*
*How did God answer Sophie?*

# A Bible Story to Remember

### Exodus 16

God heard the prayers of his people
when they were hungry and wanted
to eat. He gave them manna—a very
sweet treat! God hears every prayer and
answers in the way he thinks best. God
is never too busy to listen or hear. He
loves our words and holds them dear!

# A Prayer to Pray

*Dear God,*
*I'm so glad*
*you always hear us*
*and that you answer*
*and stay so near us.*
*Amen.*

# A Sleepy Time Activity

Let's play a listen-and-answer game!
Take turns making animal sounds.
When you know what animal it is,
answer by giving its name! As you
go to sleep, talk to God and tell him
how much you love him. He will
hear you! Night-night.

# Cool Rules

*God said, "Obey me." Jeremiah 7:23*

Max Popple and Sophie Springly were in Miss Chalkdust's class. Sophie liked school and her pretty teacher, but Max wasn't sure. "Too many rules!" frowned Max. "Put your toys away when you're done. And always remember not to run. Yuck! Too many rules!"

Miss Chalkdust said, "Rules keep us healthy and happy all day. Rules are good things we can obey!" Still, Max wasn't sure he liked so many rules.

Sophie and Max were busy in school. They learned all about letter *B* and how to count 1-2-3. They explored the science nook, fed the fish, and read a book. Then the teacher said, "It's picture painting time!"

"Oh, boy!" shouted Max, running to get his paint shirt. But in his hurry, Max tripped over the toy truck he had forgotten to pick up. He knocked his knee and spilled red paint all over his new shirt.

"Ouch!" said Max. "My knee has an owie and now so does my shirt!"

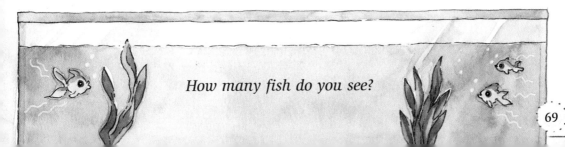

*How many fish do you see?*

Max thought about all those rules. Then Max put away the toy truck. Max cleaned up the spilled paint. Finally, Max smiled and said, "Miss Chalkdust, can we make one more rule?"

"What rule is that, Max?" asked Miss Chalkdust.

"The rule is: Whether you're at home or at school, ALWAYS obey EVERY rule!" Max said. Miss Chalkdust smiled and put the new rule on the bulletin board right then.

*Count the pencils.*
*Why should Max have followed the rules?*

# A Bible Story to Remember

### Deuteronomy 5

Night-Light has some rules to follow:
Don't fly too high and always turn your
light on in the dark. Night-Light knows
about God's rules, too. God gave Moses
ten special rules for us to obey. God
gives us rules to keep us safe at work
and play.

# A Prayer to Pray

*Dear God,*
*Please help me*
*to obey you*
*in everything*
*I say and do.*
*Amen.*

# A Sleepy Time Activity

Night-Light wants to play a game.
Think of some signs that tell us what
to do (stop sign, green light, etc.).
Tell what rules go with the signs and
how the rules keep us safe. Then
think of ways God's rules keep us
safe. Sleep tight!

# A Wrong Wish

*God said, "I will help you." Isaiah 41:10*

Sophie Springly liked everything about Mia Chang. Sophie liked Mia's shiny black hair, her striped swing set, and her pet parrot, Kei-Kei. But best of all, Sophie liked Mia's new bracelet. "It's from China," said Mia. Sophie wished more than anything to have that bracelet!

One day Sophie saw something sparkly in her yard. It was Mia's bracelet! It must have fallen off when she and Sophie were playing the other day. How it sparkled! Sophie ran to her room to try it on. Sophie thought that bracelet was the prettiest one in the world. It won't hurt if I keep it a little longer, she thought.

After school the next day, Mia called across the yard to Sophie. Sophie quickly ducked into her house. Why didn't she want to see Mia? Weren't they friends? Sophie felt funny inside. She decided to put the bracelet on again. That would make her feel better, wouldn't it?

But it didn't. The bracelet didn't seem so sparkly now. The pretty beads didn't make Sophie happy anymore. Now Sophie didn't wish for a bracelet—she wished she knew what to do!

*How many birds can you find?*

73

Could God help Sophie? Sophie prayed and thought about what God would want her to do. Then Sophie ran to Mia's house.

"My bracelet!" said Mia, when she saw what was in Sophie's hand. "I thought it was lost!" Mia said and slipped the sparkly bracelet on her wrist.

Sophie smiled. "It's such a pretty bracelet, Mia— when *you* wear it! C'mon! Let's play on your swing set!"

*Who is hiding under the bushes?*
*How did God help Sophie?*

# A Bible Story to Remember

Joshua 6:1-20

Who helped Joshua bring down the Jericho wall? God helped Joshua make the wall take a fall. And God will help us, too—even with things that seem very hard! God can help us not to be jealous, and to want good things that will help others instead of hurting them.

# A Prayer to Pray

*Dear God,*
*Please help me to see*
*what's good and right,*
*and to do what's best*
*in your sight.*
*Amen.*

# A Sleepy Time Activity

God can help you want good things for others. Think of some people, then pray for good things for them. You can pray for joy for your mommy. Or pray for love for your brother. Night-Light wishes a peaceful night for you! Good night!

# Dandy Candy

*God said, "Love your neighbor." Leviticus 19:18*

Jimmy Lopez lived in the blue house on the corner. He was seven years old and the big kid on the block. Jimmy liked to share his pony, Schnickelfritz, with his friends. He let them have bouncy rides on the pony's scruffy back.

One sunny day, Jimmy rode Schnickelfritz to Mr. Morisky's store to look at all the delicious candy. Mmmm, he wanted to taste it all! Jimmy rushed home and shook his piggy bank. Clinkety-clink. A pile of coins fell onto his floor. "I can buy LOTS of candy with this!" Jimmy said.

And so he did. He bought chocolate drops and peppermint twirls, lemony lollipops and sugary swirls. My, oh my, what a lot of candy! Then Jimmy saw his friends walking down the street. He said, "They'll want too much of my candy treat! Then what will be left for me to eat?" So he quickly started gobbling up his sweet snacks.

"Ummm-ooohhh!" groaned Jimmy after a bit. "I don't feel good. I think I feel sick! I was greedy eating all of this sticky goo. I should have shared like God wants me to!"

*Count the pets and people.*

Jimmy gathered the candy that was left and went to share it with Max, Polly, Sam, Sophie, and Mia. Then they all shared jolly, jaunty pony rides. And do you know what? Jimmy felt better right away!

"Now I know why sharing is dandy. It's the good feeling inside that's sweeter than candy!" said Jimmy. And all the friends laughed—even Schnickelfritz!

*Whose pets are on leashes?*
*How did Jimmy show love to his friends?*

# A Bible Story to Remember
## Ruth 1

Ruth and Naomi were good friends.
They helped and shared with one
another and showed God's love to each
other. God has given us lots of things,
but not just to keep for ourselves! Oh,
no! That's not neighborly! When we
take the time to share, we spread God's
love and show we care!

# A Prayer to Pray

*Dear God,*
*Please help me always*
*to give and share,*
*and spread your warm love*
*everywhere!*
*Amen.*

# A Sleepy Time Activity

Let's play a quiet game. Put your
hand over your heart and name a
person and one thing you can share.
Maybe a cookie with your sister? Feel
your heart beat and remember that
God always shares his love with us.
Night-night!

# Listen Up!

*God said, "Listen to me." Isaiah 51:1*

Mia Chang liked to help. She helped Mommy clean Kei-Kei's birdcage. She helped Daddy sweep the garage. Sometimes she helped Stormy, her kitten, find his jingle-bell ball. Today, Mommy asked her to do a special job and Mia felt very grown-up!

"You can give Kei-Kei a cracker when you hear him squawk and you can give baby Joe his bottle when you hear him fuss. But you'll have to listen carefully!" said Mommy. Mia said, "I will listen and I will help!"

Mia put the cracker and bottle on a table and sat down to listen. She heard many sounds. *Clink-clink* went the dishes in the sink. *Vroom-oom* went Mommy's vacuum in the living room. *Grick-gruck* went the big tires on the mailman's truck. Then, Mia heard "WAAAA-eeee!" What was that? Mia listened as hard as her ears would listen. Then she snatched up the cracker and the bottle.

*Find milk in three places.*

When Mommy came to see how everything was, she laughed and hugged Mia. "You listened so well to every sound—but you got Kei-Kei and Joe all turned around!" said Mommy. And sure enough, Mia had given Joe the cracker and Kei-Kei the baby bottle!

Mia laughed while Mommy cuddled baby Joe. "I listened with my ears with all of my might, but next time I'll make sure my hands get it right!" Mia giggled and gave Kei-Kei his cracker.

*Count all the birds.*
*How did Mia show that she was listening?*

# A Bible Story to Remember
## I Samuel 3

It's important to listen carefully to directions. And it's very important to listen to God! The Bible tells us that when God spoke to Samuel, Samuel listened. We can listen to God, too! God talks to us through our prayers and through his Word, the Bible.

# A Prayer to Pray

*Dear God,*
*Help me listen*
*to you every day*
*and show that I've heard you*
*by how I obey.*
*Amen.*

# A Sleepy Time Activity

Let's play a listening game. Take turns whispering words or making sounds, then echoing them back. Listen carefully! Then as you go to sleep, listen to what God says to you. He loves you! Sleep tight.

# Pretty Pony

*God said, "The Lord looks at the heart." 1 Samuel 16:7*

Today was the Pretty Pet Show and Jimmy Lopez was taking Schnickelfritz. "He's the prettiest pet there is!" said Jimmy proudly to Sam Springly. Sam said, "I don't know if he's pretty, but he sure is chubby!" Schnickelfritz nuzzled Sam and Poochie. "And he's as nice as nice can be!" laughed Sam.

Such a lot of pets were there that day. Look—there's a puppy and kitten at play. There's a lizard, a fish in a bowl, and even a hedgehog—he's adorable!

"Schnickelfritz just has to win the prize for the best pet!" Jimmy said. Finally, the contest judge came to see Schnickelfritz. The judge frowned and looked over the scruffy pony. "Well, he seems pretty chubby for a pony, I see—and his coat isn't as glossy as it could be. His tail is a bit of a tangle, you know? Still there's something about him—but I just don't know . . ." Jimmy held his breath and waited.

*How many pets are there?*

All at once, Schnickelfritz tickled the judge's ear with a friendly whiffle, then whinnied happily. The judge scratched his ear and laughed. "Well, he may not be the prettiest pet, but he's the friendliest pony I've ever met!" smiled the judge, and he handed Jimmy a blue ribbon.

Jimmy hugged his friendly pony. "Looks aren't everything," Jimmy said with pride. "It's not so important how we look, but what we're like on the inside!"

*Who is tickling the judge's ear?*
*Why did Schnickelfritz win a ribbon?*

# A Bible Story to Remember

### I Samuel 16:1-13

When God sees us, he doesn't just look at the outside. He looks at our hearts! God looked at David's heart, and not his size, when he chose him to be king. God sees our hearts, too—what we feel, think, and dream. And what's on the inside is more beautiful than anything!

# A Prayer to Pray

*Dear God,*
*Please help me*
*always be*
*the kind of person*
*you like to see!*
*Amen.*

# A Sleepy Time Activity

Let's look at our hearts. Cut a heart out of paper. Put the heart in a picture frame or just hang it by your bed. As you go to sleep, look at your heart cutout and think of ways God can help you be beautiful on the inside. Good night!

# Sam's Bully

*God said, "I will make you strong." Isaiah 45:5*

Sam Springly was worried. "Rat" Raymond, the class bully, was picking on Sam's friends. This big boy called himself "Rat" because he liked to tease the scaredy "mice" in his class. Nobody liked Rat Raymond.

"Go ahead and run! Everyone's scared of me!" Rat called when kids ran from him.

It made Sam angry that Rat was mean to other kids. But no one could stop Rat from being such a meany, right?

That night, Sam prayed, "Dear God, there's a giant problem at school. That bully Rat Raymond is breaking every rule! Please help me be strong and know what to do, 'cuz even ol' Rat is not bigger than you!" What could Sam do? Would God help Sam be strong and wise, even though Rat was twice his size?

*Point to two striped shirts.*

The next day, Sam felt brave. At lunch he walked
right up to Rat Raymond and held out a cupcake. "Here,
Rat, it's for you! I'll be your friend if you'd like me to!"

Rat stared. "No one ever wanted to be my friend," he
said. "Thanks! And by the way, my real name's Rick."

Suddenly the giant meany disappeared. Sam learned
that Rick Raymond was a nice guy! And what else did Sam
learn? No problem is too big for our God above—just look
what can happen when we share his love!

*What did Sam share?*
*Who helped Sam be strong, brave, and wise?*

# A Bible Story to Remember
## I Samuel 17:1-50

When David brought down the giant
Goliath with just a stone, he discovered
that God is bigger than anything or
anyone! When we're worried or afraid,
all we have to do is ask for God's help.
God loves us. He will answer by helping
us be strong, wise, and brave!

# A Prayer to Pray

*Dear God,*
*Thank you for being*
*faithful and true.*
*No problem is ever*
*too big for you!*
*Amen.*

# A Sleepy Time Activity

Would you like to play a game with
Night-Light? Take turns naming big
and small things. As you go to sleep,
thank God that no problem is too big
or small for him! Night-night!

# Thanks from the Heart

*God said, "Show thanks to God." Psalm 50:14*

Valentine's Day was near and the neighborhood kids were excited! "Let's do something different this year," said Max. Mia jumped up and said, "Maybe we could make the biggest valentine in the world and give it to someone who's never had a valentine!"

"But everyone has had a valentine!" said Sophie.

The kids thought for a moment, then Jimmy Lopez said, "You know, God invented love but I don't think *he's* ever had a valentine."

"That's sad," said Sophie. "I know! Let's give God the biggest valentine there ever was! We can tell God we love him and thank him for his love, too!"

The group got to work right away. The kids colored and cut and snipped hearts all day; they painted and pasted—it was more fun than play! They cut pretty pink ribbons and fancy white laces until the love in that card matched the love on their faces!

*Count the hearts.*

Then they wrote a thank-you note to God. Here's what it said:

"Dear God, it's almost Valentine's Day,
And there's something special we want to say.
No one says it quite enough
When they're saying all that mushy stuff—
But we want to give our thanks to you
For all you say and all you do!
Thank you for our families and sunshine above—
But most of all, thank you for inventing love!"
Love, Mia, Max, Jimmy, Sophie, and Sam

*How did the friends thank God?*
*Who is shown on the thank-you note?*

# A Bible Story to Remember
### Psalm 23

The Bible tells us that David worshiped and thanked God for all the things he did for him. Think of all the nice things God does for us! He has given us loving friends and families, his words in the Bible, and so much more. Let's thank God and say, "We love you!"

# A Prayer to Pray

*Dear God,*
*I give my thanks to you*
*today and through*
*my whole life, too.*
*Amen.*

# A Sleepy Time Activity

Night-Light wants to play a quiet game. Cut out five paper hearts. Take turns holding the hearts and naming things to be thankful for. As you fall asleep, hold the hearts and tell God how much you love him. Sleep tight!

# Wise Buys!

*God said, "I will give you wisdom." 1 Kings 3:12*

Max's grandpa gave him five dollars for his birthday. Max felt rich! He had seen a red race car with shiny wheels at Mr. Morisky's store. "Now I can buy it!" said Max, and he whistled and skipped all the way to the store.

"Hello, Max!" smiled Mr. Morisky. "Going to look at that race car again?" But Max said, "Not today! Today I'm going to *buy* that race car!"

When Max reached the toy aisle, he froze. A little boy was holding Max's race car! *That's my car!* Max wanted to shout. Then Max looked closely at the boy. His jeans were patched and his jacket was worn. His mommy had only a few groceries in the basket and her coat was old, too.

"It is a wonderful car, Andy. But we need these groceries instead," said the woman. "I'm sure one day you'll have a car just like it."

Max had a choice and needed God's help. "God," said Max, "I like that car but that boy does, too. Please help me be smart and know what to do!"

*Count the baskets.*

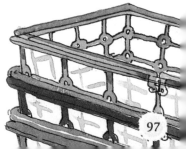

God spoke to Max's heart in a soft voice and gave Max wisdom to make the wise choice. Max walked right up to the counter. "Mr. Morisky, I'd like to buy the race car for that little boy!" Max pointed secretly to Andy.

Mr. Morisky smiled and said, "Max, you're rich with loving kindness." Max gave Mr. Morisky the money and shrugged his shoulders. "All I did was ask God for some loving 'wiseness'!" Max said as he left the store, feeling like he owned a million cool race cars!

*Count the balls in the box.*
*Why did Max need God's help and wisdom?*

# A Bible Story to Remember

I Kings 3:1-15

King Solomon asked God to make him wise. He knew that God was much wiser than anyone and always knew just what to do. God was so happy with Solomon's choice, he gave Solomon great wisdom and honor. So when you need to make a choice, trust the wisdom God gives you!

# A Prayer to Pray

*Dear Lord,*
*Please give me wisdom*
*wise and true*
*so I can make*
*good choices, too.*
*Amen.*

# A Sleepy Time Activity

Night-Light wants to make wise choices, too. Which of these actions are wise: lying? telling the truth? obeying? disobeying? praying? not going to church? As you go to sleep, think of how God's wisdom is like a special gift to you! Good night.

# An Answer in Time!

*God said, "I will answer you." Jeremiah 33:3*

Mia Chang felt awful. Grandma couldn't come to Mia's dance recital on Saturday. Grandma's car was broken and she lived two hours away.

"I'm sorry, Mia," said Grandma on the phone. "I really wanted to see my chick-a-baby dance! Maybe if we pray, God will find a way to get me there," she said. Mia loved Grandma and wanted to see her. And Mia especially wanted Grandma to see her pretty dance costume. But could God fix Grandma's car if they prayed?

"God answers prayers," Sophie Springly said to Mia. "I learned that in Sunday school! Why don't you pray?"

So Mia prayed, "Dear God, I love my Grandma so; I want to see her, don't you know? But Grandma lives away so far—could you please fix her car? Amen."

Mia prayed and prayed. Then Mia waited and waited for God to answer. Monday, Tuesday, Wednesday's near; Thursday, Friday, Saturday's here! Would God really answer? Did God really hear?

*What animals do you see?*

On Saturday afternoon, Mia was still waiting for God's answer. She put on her pretty pink-and-purple dance costume and was ready to leave the house when . . . Grandma arrived!

"My car is still broken and just won't go, so I took a bus to come see your show!" laughed Grandma. "Wow!" Mia shouted. "God did hear my prayer and he answered, too! Thank you, God—and Grandma, I love you!"

*Count the pink flowers.*
*Tell how God answered Mia's prayers.*

# A Bible Story to Remember
### Daniel 6

God promises to hear our prayers and to answer them. God answered Daniel's prayers and kept him safe in the lion's den. God will answer us in his own way—but not always the way we think he will. God's answers are never late; his answers are perfect and worth the wait!

# A Prayer to Pray

*Dear God,*
*I'm glad you answer prayer*
*and that you're always there.*
*Help me not to worry or fret—*
*Your answers are the best to get!*
*Amen.*

# A Sleepy Time Activity

Night-Light wants to draw a picture and you can, too. Draw a picture of something you pray for and want God to answer. Then say a prayer and thank God for the answer that he will send you. Night-night.

# Up a Tree!

*God said, "Be strong and brave." Joshua 1:7*

Jimmy Lopez didn't like to climb trees. He had climbed a tree once and gotten stuck. It was embarrassing! "No trees for me! Being on Schnickelfritz is as high as I'll be!" Jimmy would say.

One Saturday, Mia and her kitten, Stormy, came to see Jimmy. The sun was out and birds sang in the apple trees. Jimmy let Mia and Stormy ride Schnickelfritz around the yard. My, what fun they had, until Stormy saw a bird! Quick as a wink, the fluffy black kitten scampered up the tree.

"Stormy!" called Mia. "You come down right away!" But Stormy didn't move. Stormy was stuck! "Meeowww!" cried Stormy.

"Oh, my poor kitty—you look so blue! Jimmy, he's stuck! What will we do?" said Mia. Jimmy gulped. He was scared to climb trees—even short ones! Who could help Jimmy be strong and brave? Jimmy talked quietly to God. "Could you make me brave, God? Would you stay with me? I need to be brave to climb up this tree!"

*Count the birds.*

Then Jimmy took a deep breath and trusted God.
Jimmy kneeled on Schnickelfritz and got a boost, then
climbed and stretched until he reached Stormy in his
leafy roost! Jimmy carried Stormy down the tree and
safely into Mia's arms.

Mia hugged Stormy and said, "Thank you, Jimmy!
You're as brave as can be!"

"That's 'cuz God was climbing with me!" smiled
Jimmy.

*What animals do you see?*
*How did trusting God help Jimmy?*

# A Bible Story to Remember

Esther 4:9–5:8; 7

Because God helped Queen Esther to be brave, she was able to keep his people safe. We can trust God to make us brave, too! God doesn't want us to be afraid when he is here to help us. We just need to ask for God's help and then trust in his power and strength!

# A Prayer to Pray

*Dear God,*
*Thank you for making me*
*strong every day.*
*And help me keep trusting*
*in you every way.*
*Amen.*

# A Sleepy Time Activity

Night-Light wants to play a quiet game. Take turns telling things you're worried about or afraid of, and then say, "God said, 'Be strong and brave.'" As you fall asleep, thank God for being strong and for helping you be brave, too! Sleep tight.

# Lost and Found

*God said, "I will answer you." Jeremiah 33:3*

Sophie Springly was forgetful. Sometimes she forgot to brush her teeth. Sometimes she forgot to say thank-you. And one time, she even forgot to put on her socks! "Sophie, you'd forget your ponytail if it wasn't tied on your head!" laughed Daddy. Sophie's big brother, Sam, snickered at the idea of Sophie losing her ponytail.

One morning Mommy handed Sophie her school lunch money. "Put it someplace safe, Sophie. Don't forget!" Mommy said, as she kissed Sophie goodbye. Sophie pulled on her boots, coat, and mittens and set off for school with her best friend, Max Popple.

At school, Max and Sophie took off their mittens and hung up their coats. "I have my lunch money in this secret pocket on my new backpack," said Max. "Want to see?" Lunch money? thought Sophie. Where is *my* lunch money?

"Max, your backpack is neat—I like it a lot—but I can't find my money. I think I forgot!" Sophie peeked in her pockets and searched everywhere; she unpacked her backpack, but no money was there.

*Count all the pockets.*

"Don't worry," said Max. "Ask God for help. He knows everything. Even where your lunch money is!"

So Sophie sat down and prayed for God's help. But would God really listen? Sophie took off one boot and then the other. Then plink, plunk, clinkety-clunk—such a happy sound! Sophie's lunch money finally was found. "Oh, Max!" laughed Sophie. "God did hear me! God helped me find my money. And I did remember to keep my money safe. I just forgot that I remembered!"

*How many coins does Sophie have?*
*Who heard and answered Sophie's prayer for help?*

# A Bible Story to Remember

### Jonah 1–3

Jonah disobeyed God. But God heard Jonah's prayers and forgave him. Then he even saved him! When we trust God to hear and help us, we can forget our worries! God is listening whenever you fret, so trust in God's help and never forget!

# A Prayer to Pray

*Dear God,*
*Please let me remember*
*that you're always here*
*to listen and love me*
*and forever stay near.*
*Amen.*

# A Sleepy Time Activity

Let's play a remembering game. Look around your room for one minute, then close your eyes and tell everything you remember seeing. Now remember what God said he would do when we call. ("I will answer you.") Good night!

# I'm With You!

*God said, "I am with you." Jeremiah 30:11*

Mia was sad. Her daddy was going away on a trip. It would be four whole days before she would see Daddy again. Monday, Tuesday, Wednesday, Thursday—could she stand having Daddy away?

"Why can't I go with you?" Mia asked as Daddy packed. Daddy smiled. "Because I need you to be my helper here at home and keep Mommy and Joe from being lonesome!" he said, hugging Mia.

"But who will keep *me* from being lonesome?" sniffed Mia. Then Daddy pulled an unusual coin from his special box. The coin had tiny bits of red, yellow, and green on one side. It was a beautiful coin!

"When I was a little boy, Grandma gave me this coin when I felt lonesome. Now I think I'll give it to you!" said Daddy. "If you keep this coin and hold on to it tight, you can feel like I'm with you when I'm not in sight!"

Mia felt a little better. But would it feel like Daddy was *really* there with her?

*Point to Daddy's suitcase.*

Monday, Mia squeezed the coin all day. Tuesday, she flipped the coin to play. Wednesday, Mia took the coin to school and all the kids thought it was cool! Thursday, Mia shined the coin with care and before she knew it, Daddy was there!

"I had fun with our special coin, Daddy, and you were right! Even though you were far away, it felt like you were here each day!" shouted Mia, and she squeezed her coin and her Daddy.

*How did Daddy help Mia even though he was away?*
*Point to Mia's special coin.*

# A Bible Story to Remember
### Luke 2:4-7

The Bible tells us that God sent his Son, Jesus, to be born in a stable. God gave us Jesus to be with us and to remind us that he is here helping us. When we love God and Jesus, we're never alone!

# A Prayer to Pray

*Dear God,*
*Thank you for*
*your loving care*
*and for sending Jesus*
*to always be there!*
*Amen.*

# A Sleepy Time Activity

Let's play a quiet game. Pass a gift bow back and forth and take turns naming gifts God brings us through Jesus such as love, help, and faith. Then cuddle your bow as you think of how God and Jesus are with you even when you sleep! Night-night.

# Tied Up in Knots

*Jesus said, "Learn from me." Matthew 11:29*

"I can't do this!" pouted Sophie Springly. "I need someone to teach me!" Sophie was learning to tie her shoes—or at least, she was *trying* to learn.

"Wear slip-ons," suggested Mia Chang, showing Sophie her new shoes. "Wear cowboy boots!" shouted Jimmy Lopez, trotting by on Schnickelfritz. But Sophie wanted to tie her shoes herself. Sophie sighed as Poochie gave her a friendly lick. "You're lucky you don't wear shoes, Poochie!" said Sophie, patting her furry friend.

"I'll teach you," said Sam, sitting beside his sister. Sophie wrinkled her nose. "You, a *teacher*?" she asked. "But you're just a kid!"

"Jesus taught others once when he was just a kid!" said Sam. "Just listen to me and follow the directions." Then Sam told Sophie a story of a funny bunny with two shoelace ears.

*Who's playing with Sophie's shoelace?*

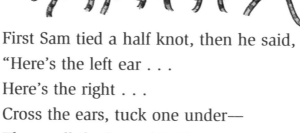

First Sam tied a half knot, then he said,
"Here's the left ear . . .
Here's the right . . .
Cross the ears, tuck one under—
Then pull the bow tight!"

Then Sophie tried. "Hmmm . . . Cross the ears, tuck one under and pull it through . . . Look, Sam! I tied my shoe!" Sam cheered and Poochie wagged all over. "When you listen to teaching that's right on the dot, the questions you have won't tie you in knots!" laughed Sam.

*Count all the ears you see.*
*What did Sam teach Sophie?*

# A Bible Story to Remember

### Luke 2:41-52

Jesus is our best teacher! Even when Jesus was young, he taught others at the temple about God and his love. Jesus was sent from God above to teach us about forgiveness and love. Jesus wants us to learn from him, too, and obey every lesson in all we do!

# A Prayer to Pray

*Dear Jesus,*
*I thank you for*
*your lessons in love*
*and all that you teach me*
*of my Father above!*
*Amen.*

# A Sleepy Time Activity

You can play a quiet learning game with Night-Light. See if you can learn this Scripture verse. Jesus said, "Learn from me" (Matthew 11:29). As you go to sleep, thank Jesus for being our best teacher—and our best friend! Sleep tight.

# In a Pickle!

*Jesus said, "Do all things that are right." Matthew 3:15*

Max Popple was excited. Today was Aunt Martha's surprise birthday party. Mommy wanted everything just right! Max helped set the table with the best dishes while Mommy poured the cake batter into the pans. Everything looked so nice. "Please put the pickles on the table, Max," said Mommy as she went to answer the phone. But when Max picked up the pickle dish, out popped a pickle into a pan of cake batter!

"Uh-oh," said Max, quickly trying to think what to do. But before he could decide, Mommy came back and whisked the cake pans into the oven. "There!" smiled Mommy. "Now everything is just right!"

But not *everything* was right! Max thought about that little pickle and worried. "If I tell Mommy now she might be mad and Aunt Martha's surprise will be awfully bad. Maybe the pickle will melt and just go. I won't say a word and then no one will know!" But Max knew. And God knew, too. Would Max do the right thing, like God would want him to?

*Count the pickles.*

After dinner, Aunt Martha blew out the birthday candles. Mommy cut the cake. And Max held his breath. That little pickle is there in the cake, he thought. Nobody knows I made a mistake! But someone did know. Max knew. He felt awful. He knew he had not done the right thing. What should he do? Was it too late?

Then Max told the truth. He said he was sorry. Did Mommy get mad? No, not at all—absolutely not! Instead she forgave Max right on the spot. And no, Aunt Martha's surprise was not *just* right. But Aunt Martha laughed, "Pickle-cake! I think I'll try a bite!"

*Count the candles.*
*What did Max do that was wrong?*

# A Bible Story to Remember
### Matthew 3:13-17

Max did the right thing when he told the truth. The Bible tells us that Jesus did the right thing when he was baptized. It's good for us to do what's right, too—what's good and kind in Jesus' sight. When we do good things in love, we know God smiles from above!

# A Prayer to Pray

*Dear God,*
*Please help me always*
*to be just like you*
*and choose the right thing*
*in all that I do.*
*Amen.*

# A Sleepy Time Activity

Night-Light wants to play a game. Take turns making up choices and deciding what's the right thing to do. Tell a lie or tell the truth? Pick up your toys or leave a mess? As you fall asleep, think about the right things that Jesus did. Good night!

# Follow the Leader

*Jesus said, "Follow me." Matthew 4:19*

It was a lovely summer day, just right for any kind of play! "Let's play Follow the Leader!" cried Jimmy Lopez. Mia Chang, Sophie Springly, and Max and Polly Popple shouted, "Good idea!" and hopped in line behind Jimmy.

"We'll take turns being the leader," explained Jimmy. "Follow me!" Jimmy led and everyone followed. They jumped after Jimmy to a red sandbox, walked around the rim, and across big rocks.

Then Mia led and everyone followed. They skipped with Mia past a rake and hoe. They hopped over a creek bed where water once flowed.

Then Max led and everyone followed. They climbed with Max up a short, steep hill and when he tiptoed down, they followed him still!

"Now me!" squealed Polly. Polly led and everyone followed. They paraded after Polly through a sprinkler-flood—right up to a puddle of . . .

*How many frogs can you find?*

"Not *mud*!" laughed the kids. "Polly," said Sophie, "a good leader leads toward good things. C'mon, I'll show you how!" Sophie led and everyone followed. They marched after Sophie as best as they were able—right into her house and straight to the table.

"Pizza!" shouted the kids. Sophie's daddy had just set a freshly baked pizza out to cool. "Leading toward good things is what a good leader knows—and though I was the leader, I just followed my nose!" Sophie said.

*Count the cups.*
*Tell what a good leader does.*

# A Bible Story to Remember

### Matthew 4:18-20

Jesus leads us toward all good things
such as love, forgiveness, eternal life,
and faith. Jesus called special disciples
to follow him. Now Jesus wants us to
follow him, too. What a loving leader
to follow!

# A Prayer to Pray

*Dear God,*
*Please help me follow*
*only you*
*and stick to your way*
*my whole life through.*
*Amen.*

# A Sleepy Time Activity

Night-Light wants to play a quiet
game of Follow the Leader! Follow
these directions: touch your nose;
pat your toes; count to five; clap
your hands three times; say "I'll
follow Jesus!" Think of how nice
it is to follow Jesus! Night-night.

# Snowman McGee

*Jesus said, "Love each other." John 13:34*

What a lot of snow! Jolly snowmen were all over town. Why, the kids even made a snowman in grouchy old Mr. McGee's yard. "Snowmen—bahhh!" grumbled Mr. McGee as he shoveled his snowy sidewalk.

"You know, I don't think he's really that grouchy," said Sam Springly. "He's just not happy much."

"Maybe that's because he's cold and can't afford a warm coat," said Jimmy Lopez. "I saw him shivering at the bus stop the other day!"

"The Helpers Club could help," suggested Sam. "We could show Mr. McGee that we like him and we care!" After a little thinking, the Helpers Club had a wonderful idea. Everyone ran home to get a special secret surprise. What were they up to? How were they going to show Mr. McGee they cared?

*Count the snowman's pebbles.*

Sam brought Daddy's warm old coat and Mia brought her fuzzy scarf. Sophie added her daddy's brown boots, and Max his red hat just for hoots! Jimmy slipped on mittens, left and right; then the snowman was done—and oh, what a sight! Mr. McGee stepped outside, looking a little mean. But all of a sudden he laughed out loud and said, "That's the funniest snowman I've ever seen!"

He smiled at the helpers. "Thank you for your gift of love. Now let's all warm up with hot cocoa in mugs!"

*Point to everything that is blue.*
*How did the kids show love to Mr. McGee?*

# A Bible Story to Remember
### Matthew 5:43-48

Jesus spent his life loving others and
being kind and caring. Everywhere he
went he told people to love one another.
Jesus wants us to love one another, too.
We can show our love through hugs,
kind words, and praying for others. How
do you show your love?

# A Prayer to Pray

*Dear God,*
*Help us always*
*be kind to others*
*and find new ways*
*to love one another.*
*Amen.*

# A Sleepy Time Activity

Before you go to sleep, do some of
these loving things: hug somebody;
say something kind; give a loving
pat; give someone a good-night
kiss. As you go to sleep, think of
how you can show Jesus your love!
Sleep tight.

# Fear Not!

*Jesus said, "Don't be afraid." Matthew 10:31*

Max Popple was afraid of his new piano. "Afraid of a piano? That's silly!" said Sophie Springly. Max frowned. "Well, I'm not 'xactly afraid of the piano," he said. "I'm afraid I can't play it so good!" Max played a few notes. Plink-plunk-CRUNNKK! Sophie covered her ears. "Ouch! Maybe you could play the tuba instead," she suggested.

"I have to play my song for lots of people tomorrow," groaned Max, "to show them how my piano lessons are going." Sophie thought a bit and then said, "Max, there's only one thing to do! Invite Jesus to be there with you!"

"Invite Jesus?" asked Max. "He doesn't want to hear me play the piano!" "Sure he does!" Sophie said. "Jesus can help you not be scared and he can help you play the piano, too! We can do *everything* with Jesus' help!"

Max sat at the piano and thought as he played. Could Jesus help him not be afraid?

*Who's peeking around the corner?*

The next day, Max felt sure Jesus could help! Even though lots of people were listening, Max wasn't afraid. He just invited Jesus to be with him. Max played the piano and knew Jesus was there! And when every sweet note of his song filled the air, Max smiled and said, "I wasn't afraid with Jesus right here. And now I know faith is music to his ear!"

*Count the flowers.*
*Why did Max ask Jesus to be with him?*

# A Bible Story to Remember

### Luke 8:22-25

We're all afraid sometimes, even Jesus' special disciples. They were afraid in a very bad storm. But Jesus told them not to be afraid. Jesus can help us to not be afraid, too. When we invite Jesus into our lives, he stays with us all the time so we never have to feel alone!

# A Prayer to Pray

*Dear God,*
*Thank you for taking*
*my fears away*
*and for your loving help*
*both night and day.*
*Amen.*

# A Sleepy Time Activity

Let's make a special "Welcome" sign to invite Jesus to be with us. Use crayons and paper to draw a happy "Welcome, Jesus!" sign, then tape it beside your bed. As you go to sleep, think of how Jesus is with you. Good night!

# Achoo for You!

*Jesus said, "Help other people freely." Matthew 10:8*

Everyone in Mia Chang's class had a cold—everyone except Mia. There were snuffles and sniffles and coughs galore; there were sneezes, wheezes, whiffles, and more! Mia wanted to help everyone feel better, but what could she do? Then Mia had a great idea! When she got home, she put pretty paper and bows on a special gift box. "Now I can help my friends!" smiled Mia.

The next day, everyone wondered what Mia had in her pretty package. "It's something to help you!" was all Mia would say. Then all of a sudden, there was a snuffly sneeze—a giant ACHOO as big as you please! Mia reached for her gift box and ran to her friend.

"Here's something you need and it's just for you. It will help your sniffles and sneezy achoos!" smiled Mia.

"Thanks, Mia, that's a nice gift!" laughed her friend. All morning Mia helped her friends and in return she heard many thank-yous between the achoos. It was fun to help others!

*Find seven bows.*

When everyone had a special gift, Mia's nose began to itch. "Ah-ah-ahhhhCHOO!" she sneezed. Mia's friends ran to the gift box and pulled out a gift for Mia.

"Here's something you need and it's just for you. It will help your sniffles and sneezy achoos!" they said. They handed Mia a tissue as soft as a rose, and Mia giggled as she blew her nose.

*Why did Mia bring a gift box to school?*
*What was in Mia's gift box?*

# A Bible Story to Remember

John 6:5-14

Jesus spent his life helping other people because he loved them. He helped a big crowd of people when he fed all their hungry tummies with five loaves of bread and two small fish! Jesus wants us to help others, too. When we help others, we show them we love them.

# A Prayer to Pray

*Dear God,*
*Let me help others*
*as you taught me to.*
*Please help me be helpful*
*in all that I do.*
*Amen.*

# A Sleepy Time Activity

Take turns telling ways to help in these situations: when Daddy is hungry; when the trash is full; when Mommy has a headache; when a friend is sad. As you go to sleep, think of ways you can help others and spread Jesus' love! Night-night.

# Sophie the Samaritan

*Jesus said, "Show mercy." Luke 6:36*

It sure is hard to like everyone. Sophie Springly didn't like the new girl in her class—no, siree! The little girl broke Sophie's crayons and knocked over Sophie's building block tower. Then she scribbled on Sophie's beautiful painting! Sophie thought, I'm really mad. This is it! I don't think I like her one little bit!

Sophie had a shiny new bicycle and wanted to take it to school for show-and-tell. "Sam can walk with you," smiled Mommy. "Take care of your new bicycle!"

Sophie rode proudly, but when she reached school, the new girl ran up and said, "Your bike's really cool! Can I ride it? I can ride real good!" Before Sophie could answer, the girl rode off in a flash. But a moment later—oh, what a crash! The little girl ran into a tree, bumped the bike, and nicked her knee.

Sophie felt funny. She felt mad and a little glad. But there was another feeling Sophie had. Sophie felt sort of bad! She knew she should help the girl. But could she help someone she didn't really like?

*How many squirrels are there?*

Sophie thought about the story she'd heard in Sunday school. It was the Bible story about the man who was left hurt on the road and the good Samaritan who helped him. Sophie thought and then she decided. She *could* help that little girl! Sophie ran to help her. The surprised little girl said, "You really want to help me?"

"Sure," smiled Sophie, feeling friendlier. "You need help and I'm right here, too. I will give my help to you. I'm glad you think my bike is cool, and you can try it again after school!"

*Count the flowers.*
*Why did Sophie help the little girl?*

# A Bible Story to Remember
### Luke 10:30-37

Jesus teaches us to love and care for all people. To help us understand, Jesus told about a Samaritan man who was merciful to a stranger in need. Just like the Samaritan man, we need to be kind all the time—even to people who don't treat us very well.

# A Prayer to Pray

*Dear God,*
*Please help me*
*always be*
*kind to those*
*who are mean to me.*
*Amen.*

# A Sleepy Time Activity

Night-Light wants to play a quiet game. Say a way to be merciful and kind when someone breaks your favorite toy, or calls you a name, or pushes you. As you go to sleep, think of how Jesus loves us all the time—no matter what! Sleep tight.

# Plans for Cans

*Jesus said, "Trust in me." John 14:1*

Mr. Morisky's store was such a fun place! There were stacks of soup cans, cartons, crates, and mile-high piles of paper plates!

"It would be easy to run a store," said Jimmy Lopez. "And fun and tasty!" agreed Sam Springly, patting the Souper Soup display. Mr. Morisky chuckled as he heard the boys. "It's not as easy as you think to build these displays. You have to be able to trust your building plans!"

"Building plans just for cans?" laughed Sam. "We can stack these cans so high, they'll climb up to the sky! We don't need any building plans."

"Well, you can try, but I think you'll see what I mean," smiled Mr. Morisky. "You need building plans you can trust!" So Jimmy and Sam went to work. They built a tower 1-2-3, and made it as tall as it could be! Then they stood back and smiled proudly. "We don't need building plans! We can just stack up all the cans!" they said.

*How many cans did Sam stack?*

Then a boy grabbed a can for his mommy. The tower of cans started to sway, and soon the whole stack just gave way! BANG! Down came all the cans in a clattering roar, scattering all over Mr. Morisky's floor!

"Wow!" said Sam, "You were right, Mr. Morisky!"

Mr. Morisky put his hand on Sam's shoulder. "When you build, you need a base you can trust. You use one that's solid, that's really a must! That's why we need to build our lives with Jesus in our hearts. His rock-solid love won't let us fall apart!"

*Why did the boys' stack of cans fall down?*
*Who's picking up the cans?*

# A Bible Story to Remember

### Matthew 7:24-27

Jesus told about two builders. One man was foolish and built his house on sand. But the other man was wise. He built his house on rock. We are wise when we build our lives around Jesus. We can trust Jesus to help us live and love in the best way.

# A Prayer to Pray

*Dear God,
Please help me have
more trust in you
and build my life
around you, too.
Amen.*

# A Sleepy Time Activity

Let's play a quiet building game. Take turns stacking blocks or plastic cups. For each one, name a way Jesus helps us. As you go to sleep, think of how good it feels to trust in Jesus! Good night.

# Poochie's Lost!

*Jesus said, "I will be with you always." Matthew 28:20*

Poochie didn't like his new collar and tags. His name tag jingled. His address tag jangled. Poochie tried to scratch that collar off—but it wouldn't budge.

"When you wear your collar, it's almost like we're there with you, keeping you safe and loving you, too!" Sam told Poochie. But Poochie just shook his head.

One pretty day, Poochie ran outside to play. He snuffled the grass and the morning frost, he scampered and ran until—oh, no!—he was lost.

"Poochie!" called Sam. "Here, Poochie-boy!" called Sophie. They looked here, they searched there, but Poochie wasn't anywhere!

They went home with sad faces. "I know he's just one small pup," said Sam sadly, "but I love him so much—I can't give him up!"

"He's wearing his collar and tags," said Sophie hopefully. "That's right," said Mommy. "Just as God is with us and helps us stay safe and sound, Poochie's collar is with him, too, and will help him to be found!"

*Point to Poochie's pictures.*

Just then the doorbell rang and Sam heard a "Woof!" Could Poochie really be at the door? Was Poochie found and home once more?

"Woof-woof!" Poochie barked when he saw Sam. The lady holding Poochie laughed. "Your pup is happy to be home! I saw your address on his collar."

"Oh, thank you!" shouted Sam as he hugged Poochie. "There's lots of dogs in the world, that's true—but not one is as special to me as you!"

*Who is Poochie happy to see?*
*Why was this one dog so important to Sam?*

# A Bible Story to Remember

### Luke 15:3-7

It's so good to know that God cares for each of us and is always with us. The Bible tells us that God is like a shepherd who loves his sheep and wants them close to him all the time. God loves us so much, he knows where we are and stays with us every moment!

# A Prayer to Pray

*Dear God,*
*I'm so glad*
*you're always here*
*and that your love*
*is always near.*
*Amen.*

# A Sleepy Time Activity

Night-Light wants to have some flashlight fun. Look around your room, then turn off the lights. Shine the flashlight on one thing that you know is still with you even at night. Snuggle up and think of how Jesus is there loving you. Night-night.

# Step by Step

*Jesus said, "Trust in me." John 14:1*

Baby Joe was growing. He could sit up by himself and take drinks from his sipper cup. And baby Joe could skitter across the floor on his tummy. But Mia was excited to have her baby brother learn to walk.

"C'mon, baby," encouraged Mia. "You can do it!" But each time Joe tried to walk, he just teetered, tottered, and tumbled right over! "You can learn, you really must. I just need to help you trust!" said Mia. Then Mia gathered Joe's favorite toys and put them in a row across the floor.

First came Joe's cute stuffed goat, then his bathtub sailing boat. Next came his teddy bear, and finally his fun yellow chair. Joe was excited to see all of his favorite toys. He tried to get up, but he just plopped down with a thump. He tried to pull himself up on a little table, but— oh, no!—he just wasn't able.

Then Mia took the baby's tiny hands in hers. "You can do it, baby brother. I know you can. Here, you can start by holding my hand!" Mia walked a few steps with Joe, then, oh . . . oh . . . OH!

*What's under the table?*

155

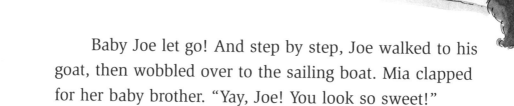

Baby Joe let go! And step by step, Joe walked to his goat, then wobbled over to the sailing boat. Mia clapped for her baby brother. "Yay, Joe! You look so sweet!"

Joe trusted Mia—and his feet! He toddled over to his teddy bear, then step by step to his yellow chair. Baby Joe clapped and stomped his baby feet happily. Mia hugged Joe. "You learned to walk and to trust, Joe! Having trust is like a test—you did so well, now sit and rest!" And that's just what he did!

*How many stars can you find?*
*What did Mia do to help Joe learn to trust?*

# A Bible Story to Remember

### Matthew 9:1-8

The Bible tells of some friends who trusted Jesus to make their friend walk again, and he did! We learn to trust by seeing how Jesus loves us, helps us, and answers our prayers. Step by step—now that's the way—bit by bit we trust Jesus each day.

# A Prayer to Pray

*Dear God,*
*Help me trust you*
*more each day*
*with all I do*
*and all I say.*
*Amen.*

# A Sleepy Time Activity

Night-Light wants to play a quiet game. Name some things you have learned to do such as walking, riding a bicycle, or skipping. Then tell how trust helped you learn. As you go to sleep, think of how sweet it is to trust in Jesus. Sleep tight!

# Everyone's Invited

*Jesus said, "Come to me." Matthew 19:14*

Sophie and Mia were planning a tea party. They planned to set the table with their best plastic tea sets. They planned to serve graham crackers with icing and candy sprinkles. And they planned to pour apple juice from their fancy teapot.

"Mommy says we can't have tea, so juice sounds just as good to me!" smiled Sophie. "But who can we invite?"

The girls thought for a moment. Then Mia said, "We won't invite babies 'cuz they cry a lot. And they might tip over the tea party pot!"

"And we won't invite grown-ups to sip tea or eat, 'cuz they might not like our sprinkly treats!" added Sophie.

"What about boys?" asked Mia.

"Boys?" said Sophie. "We won't invite boys to our afternoon tea—they don't know how to sip tea politely!"

"Who can we invite?" wondered Mia. "There's nobody left!"

*Count the plates and cups.*

BABIES
BIG PEOPLE
BOYS
EVERYONE!

The girls thought and thought. Then Sophie said, "Who would Jesus invite to a party or tea? Surely he would invite everyone he'd see!"

Mia smiled and nodded. "If Jesus would invite everyone, including you and me, then we'll invite everyone to our neighborhood tea!" she said.

"Well, if we're going to invite everyone in the neighborhood," laughed Sophie, "we'd better get a bigger teapot!"

*How many bracelets do you see?*
*Who did the girls invite to come to their party?*

# A Bible Story to Remember

### Matthew 19:13-15

Jesus showed his love when he told the children to come to him. Jesus loves us all and wants us all to know and follow him. He invites us all to come and learn about our Father above—young or old or shy or bold—Jesus wants everyone to share his love!

# A Prayer to Pray

*Dear God,*
*I'm so glad*
*you want me near*
*and like to be*
*with me right here!*
*Amen.*

# A Sleepy Time Activity

Night-Light wants to play a quiet game. Pretend you're going to have a party with Jesus and name all the people you would invite! As you go to sleep, think about how much Jesus wants you to share his love! Good night.

# Forgiving Friends

*Jesus said, "Forgive other people." Luke 6:37*

Max Popple was making valentines—the very special homemade kind! Max made a valentine heart to exchange with everyone in his class, but the prettiest one he made was for Sophie Springly.

"Sophie is my best friend in the world—even if she is a girl!" said Max, adding the finishing touches to the lacy heart. "Sophie will like this valentine a lot!" Max couldn't wait until Sophie saw it.

At party time, the kids put valentine cards on their friends' desks. Max peeked at Sophie. When would she see his card? But when Sophie finally did look at Max, she wasn't smiling. She didn't look happy at all!

"What's wrong, Sophie?" asked Max. Sophie frowned. "I got a card from everyone but you—and I thought we were best friends, too!" Sophie said, and walked away in a huff. Max gulped. Something had gone wrong! What had he done? Would Sophie ever forgive him?

*How many cards does Max have?*

Just then Phil Finnegan laughed. "Look! I got this card that's awfully lacy—I'm pretty sure it's not for me!"

So that's what happened! Sophie's card got stuck to Phil's. Max and Sophie looked at one another and laughed. "Sophie, I'm as sorry as I can be! I put your card on the wrong desk—will you forgive me?" asked Max.

Sophie laughed and nodded her head. "I'll forgive you if you forgive me—now let's be best friends like we should be!" And they were!

*How many hearts do you see?*

# A Bible Story to Remember

### Luke 19:1-10

Zacchaeus was really kind of mean. But Jesus loved Zacchaeus, and forgave him for everything. Jesus is forgiving and he wants us to be forgiving, too. It isn't always easy, but it's always the right thing to do.

# A Prayer to Pray

*Dear God,*
*I want to be*
*just like you*
*and be forgiving*
*as you want me to.*
*Amen.*

# A Sleepy Time Activity

Take turns remembering times you needed forgiveness or you forgave someone. How did you feel? How did love help you forgive someone? As you fall asleep, think of how Jesus loves and forgives us when we ask him. Night-night!

# The Giving Flower

*Jesus said, "Give to God." Matthew 22:21*

Jimmy Lopez felt like he'd won a million dollars! He woke up to a sunshiny day full of playful breezes. Jimmy went outside and stooped to pick the prettiest flower in the garden. It was easy to love the whole world on such a lovely morning!

But not everyone was happy. Jimmy's neighbor, Mrs. Flutterby, was feeling flustered. She had burned her best cinnamon rolls. Jimmy saw her frown and went over to give Mrs. Flutterby the beautiful flower. "Here's something I can give to you—it'll help you smile the whole day through!" Jimmy said. Mrs. Flutterby laughed. "Thanks for giving me a smile!" she said happily.

From that moment on, each minute and hour, the beautiful blossom was a busy flower! It traveled here and was given there. It brought love and smiles everywhere!

Mrs. Flutterby gave the flower to her friend Mrs. Click, to give her a smile since her daughter was sick. And when sick little Sarah was feeling quite sad, her mommy gave her the flower to make her feel glad!

**Can you find six butterflies?**

167

The giving went round in a circle all day, and came back to the start when Jimmy went to play.

"I'm sorry you're sick, Sarah. I feel bad," Jimmy said. Then Sarah gave Jimmy the flower. "This will help you feel glad!" she said.

Jimmy looked at the flower, then laughed with joy. "Giving love away is easy, I've found. And when we give love to others, it comes back around!"

*How did Jimmy give to others?*
*Who gave the flower back to Jimmy?*

# A Bible Story to Remember

### Luke 21:1-4

The Bible tells of a poor woman who cheerfully gave God all she had—two copper coins. We can give cheerfully to God, too. When we give others our help, sharing, caring, and love, we are also giving to God. Giving love is easy to do, and that love will come back to you!

# A Prayer to Pray

*Dear God,*
*Please help me have*
*a loving heart.*
*That is where*
*the giving starts!*
*Amen.*

# A Sleepy Time Activity

Let's make giving flowers! Cut out a paper flower and use crayons to decorate it. As you go to sleep, look at the flower and think about all the love you can give to God. Then give your pretty flower to someone in the morning! Sleep tight.

# Ready for Beddy

*Jesus said, "Be ready." Luke 12:40*

"Bedtime for Max and Polly!" called Mommy. It was eight o'clock and time to get ready for bed. "Ready for beddy, Freddy?" asked Daddy. Max said, "Almost! I just have to finish brushing my teeth and washing my face. Getting ready for bed is a lot of work!"

"Ready for beddy, Neddy?" joked Daddy to Polly. But Polly wasn't ready for beddy. She didn't want her jammies on or slippers on her feet. Polly didn't like to wash her face or brush her teeth. Polly didn't like going to bed! She wanted to play instead. "Not ready!" said Polly stubbornly.

Max bent down and said, "But Polly, if you don't get ready now, you'll never be ready to go to sleep! And if you don't go to sleep, you can't wake up to have pancakes and bacon, and juice in your cup! And if you don't have a good breakfast, think how hungry you'll be! And if you're hungry and don't have energy, you won't be able to run and have fun! And if you don't have any energy zip, just think how sleepy you'll get! Then you'll yawn and nod your head and want to get ready to sleep in your bed!"

*Find two bears.*

171

Polly's little eyes got bigger and bigger as Max talked. As soon as Max was finished, Polly brushed her teeth and washed her face. She put her pajamas on and her pillow in place. Then she climbed into her bed and shouted, "READY FOR BEDDY!" Max and Daddy laughed. Max said, "That's right, Polly. If you get ready for bed now, you'll be ready for a fun new day tomorrow! G'night, Polly!"

"G'night, Max!" Polly said, and shut her eyes tight.

*Count the lambs.*
*Why was it important for Polly to get ready?*

# A Bible Story to Remember

### Matthew 21:6-11

Jesus was coming to Jerusalem and the people were ready! They gave him a very special welcome. It's important to be ready for Jesus! We need to be ready to obey Jesus, to serve him, and to trust him. When we're ready for Jesus, we're ready for anything!

# A Prayer to Pray

*Dear God,*
*I want to be*
*ready for you*
*and give you my love*
*my whole life through.*
*Amen.*

# A Sleepy Time Activity

Night-Light wants to play a game. Tell about everything you do to get ready for each of these: bedtime; supper time; bath time; school; church. As you fall asleep, think of how you can be ready to give Jesus your life! Good night.

# Apple Daze

*Jesus said, "Be like the servant." Luke 22:26*

The Helpers Club was at Jimmy Lopez's house. The autumn leaves drifted down to the ground as the kids enjoyed cookies and apple juice. They talked about how they could serve others. "We could rake leaves for Mr. Morisky," said Sam. Mia said, "We could collect toys to give to kids in the hospital."

"How about serving us more apple juice, Jimmy?" laughed Max, holding out his empty glass.

"Hey, that's it!" said Jimmy. "Let's serve people who are hungry by picking apples for the town food pantry! The trees in my backyard are full of good ol' apples!" Everyone cheered and Polly Popple clapped her pudgy hands. "You can serve by watching the apples, Polly," smiled Max, patting his little sister's head.

The Helpers Club picked apples all day, and piled them in piles out of the way. Red apples, yellow ones, green apples, too! The kids picked those apples until late afternoon—but what a surprise once they were through!

**Find all the baskets.**

"Polly!" said Max, "What did you do? You bit every apple almost clear through!" Sure enough, little Polly Popple had taken one big bite out of every apple. Polly smiled proudly. "Good apples!" she squealed.

"I think Polly was just serving us—as our official apple-taster!" giggled Sophie. Jimmy laughed, too. "That's OK, we can still serve. My mom will help us make lots of yummy applesauce!"

*Count the bitten apples.*
*How did the Helper's Club serve?*

# A Bible Story to Remember

### John 13:1-17; Mark 14:22-26

Jesus served his disciples by washing their feet. He wanted to show how much he loved them. There are many ways that we can serve others, too, such as doing useful things, being good listeners, and saying kind words. When we serve, we show others we care.

# A Prayer to Pray

*Dear God,*
*Please help me*
*look for ways*
*to serve and be helpful*
*all of my days.*
*Amen.*

# A Sleepy Time Activity

Let's find some apples! Draw an apple tree on a piece of paper. For each apple you draw, think of a person or a way you can serve. As you fall asleep, think about how serving others shows them your love. Night-night!

# Polly-Oops!

*Jesus said, "Forgive them." Luke 23:34*

Little Polly Popple was always dropping, bopping, bumping, breaking, and tripping over everything! "Oops," Polly said when she spilled her milk. "Oops," Polly said when she broke Mommy's vase. "Oops-oops!" Polly said when she flushed Daddy's tie down the potty. Mommy smiled patiently. "She's too little to know what's best to do," she said. Daddy laughed. "She's our little Polly-oops," he said, hugging his little girl.

Polly's brother, Max, had a remote-controlled truck. Max would hold the remote control and make the truck turn right and left, then spin around. It would go up hills and rumble down. Max loved his truck and Polly loved to watch Max drive.

One day Max was wheeling his truck across the driveway. Polly held her juice and laughed as the truck spun around her feet in funny loops. "Zoom, zoom, go!" clapped Polly. But when she clapped, down went the cup—and a very juicy truck came to a stop!

"Oops," whispered Polly. "Poll-YYYY!" Max groaned.

*What bugs do you see?*

"Look what you've done!" Max said. "You've ruined my truck and all of our fun!" Max was mad—but he also knew in his heart that Polly didn't mean to drop her juice. Max thought about how Jesus forgave others. Then Max looked deeper into his heart and knew he loved Polly, even if she caused trouble sometimes.

Polly's bottom lip was sticking out and her eyes were so, so sad. "Polly-oops," she said, as a tear slid down her cheek. Max gathered up all the love in his heart and said, "I forgive you, Polly-oops! Now let's fix our truck and do some loopy-loops!"

*Count four flowers.*
*Why did Max forgive Polly?*

# A Bible Story to Remember
### Matthew 27:11-66

Jesus died to forgive our sins and to show us God's love never ends. Jesus wants us to love and forgive, too. When we forgive with love, we grow closer to God in heaven above!

# A Prayer to Pray

*Dear God,*
*Please help me be*
*just like you*
*and show forgiveness*
*to others, too.*
*Amen.*

# A Sleepy Time Activity

(Sing to "Jesus Loves Me.")
F-O-R-G-I-V-E,
Jesus forgave you and me!
Forgiving is how we all should be—
F-O-R-G-I-V-E!
Sing this song and thank Jesus for forgiving us with love! Sleep tight.

# Love Is Alive

*Jesus said, "I will be with you always." Matthew 28:20*

Jimmy Lopez was very sad. It was Easter morning and he missed his daddy. Jimmy's daddy died when Jimmy was five. Jimmy missed him a lot. "Mommy," asked Jimmy, "why did Daddy have to die? I feel so sad inside." Mommy hugged Jimmy and said, "Jesus' friends asked the same question and felt the same way when Jesus died on the cross. They had to trust God's plans. And they had to remember all the love Jesus gave them."

"I can remember Daddy's love," said Jimmy. Mommy said, "Why don't we look at our special pictures and remember!" She got the picture book out. Jimmy pointed and said, "Here's when Daddy and I washed the car—and the time that we rode on a bus oh-so-far!"

"And remember the time we all went to the zoo?" Mommy asked. Jimmy laughed and said, "When Daddy hopped me around like a big kangaroo! And here's the day that we cooked lunch outside and Daddy gave me my first Schnickelfritz ride!"

*Point to all the pictures.*

Then Jimmy stopped and smiled. "This is like the first Easter," he said. "Jesus' friends found out that Jesus was alive and would always be with them. And now I know that even though Daddy's not alive, his memory can live with me and his love stays alive in my heart!"

Jimmy's mom smiled and said, "Let's take some time before we go to church and thank God for his love, and for giving us special memories." Then Jimmy and Mommy prayed together.

*Whose hat does Jimmy have?*
*Why was Jimmy sad?*

# A Bible Story to Remember

### Luke 24:1-12

Jesus died to forgive our sins. That was very sad. But we can be happy knowing that Jesus is alive today. He helps us in every way, even when people we love die. He helps us to trust God's plans and to remember his love.

# A Prayer to Pray

*Dear God,*
*I'm happy more than I can say because I know you're alive today! Help me to know you're always there to heal my sorrow and to care. Amen.*

# A Sleepy Time Activity

Let's play a remembering game. Take turns remembering the following times: a happy time; a time you were sick; your favorite toy; a trip you took. As you fall asleep, remember how good it is to know that Jesus is alive and loving you! Good night.

# Spread the Good News

*Jesus said, "Tell the Good News." Mark 16:15*

Sophie Springly was excited! She had good news to tell. Who could she tell her news to? Hey, there was Ginny James playing ball! Surely she'd like to hear this good news. Sophie skipped, stopped, then sat. Sophie had great news today, but what exactly would she say?

Just then, Sam Springly and Max Popple appeared. They were bouncing basketballs. "What's up, Sophie?" asked Sophie's big brother. "You look worried."

Sophie sighed and said, "I wanted to tell Ginny James my important news, but I don't know how." "What news?" Sam asked. Sophie smiled. "It's the Good News about Jesus!" she said. Then her smile faded away. "But I don't know exactly what words I should say."

"That's easy!" said Max. "Tell Ginny that Jesus is our best friend—that he stays right beside us from beginning to end!" Sam smiled and joined in, "And you can tell her about Jesus' great love, and how he was sent here from God up above!" Then Sophie shouted happily, "And Jesus forgives us and cares in every way—that's what I'll tell her! That's what I'll say!"

**Count the basketballs.**

But when Sophie jumped up and turned around, Ginny James was nowhere to be found. "Well," sighed Sophie, "guess I'll just have to tell her some other time."

What a surprise Sophie had the next day at Sunday school! Who was sitting at the front table? Ginny James!

Ginny grinned at Sophie and said, "I know you thought I was gone yesterday, but I listened to what you all had to say. And Jesus sounded so awesome, I wanted to come to church today!"

*Find three stars.*
*What good news did Sophie want to share with Ginny?*

# A Bible Story to Remember

### Mark 16:15-20

When you have good news, you want to share it, don't you? It's important for everyone to know, love, and follow Jesus. That's why Jesus told his friends to go and tell others about him. Jesus wants everyone to know he's here to forgive and love us so!

# A Prayer to Pray

*Dear God,*
*Help me to be brave*
*and always tell*
*the Good News about you*
*that I love so well!*
*Amen.*

# A Sleepy Time Activity

Night-Light wants to play an echo game and you can play, too! Take turns saying something about Jesus and having the other person repeat it! As you go to sleep, think about all the wonderful things you can tell about Jesus. Night-night!

# The Special Helper

*Jesus said, "Receive the Holy Spirit." John 20:22*

Mia was worried. Her teacher was gone and a new teacher stood in front of the boys and girls. Mia's teacher was young and had long hair. This teacher had curly grey hair and wore glasses. Where was the teacher she knew and loved?

"Miss Maypole is not feeling well today, boys and girls," said the new teacher, "but she asked me to come and be your special helper. We'll have a wonderful day, I'm sure!" But Mia wasn't sure.

At music time, they sang their favorite song, and the special helper let them clap along. At playtime, the teacher skipped rope with them all, and they laughed and giggled to see her play ball! Everyone had fun and even Mia smiled a little. Then came writing time.

Mia didn't like writing time because she had trouble making her *M's*. Mia's *M's* never stood up straight and tall—they looked more like *N's* that had taken a fall! What would this new teacher say when she saw?

*Count the children.*

"Maybe I can help," smiled the special helper. She lightly held Mia's hand and showed her how to make two mountaintops. "Make a mountain, make even two— and here's the *M* that's made by you!" she said.

Mia was amazed! The special helper had really helped her. Now Mia could make the prettiest *M's* she had ever made! She hugged the special helper. "You came as a helper; now you're my friend! You helped me to trust— and make my *M's*!" Mia said, and smiled.

*Find five pencils.*
*Who was Mia's special helper?*

# A Bible Story to Remember

### Acts 2

We all need help. Jesus sent us a
special helper—the Holy Spirit. When
we accept Jesus, the Holy Spirit lives
in us and helps us do right things.
The Holy Spirit loves us and gives us
strength! Isn't our special helper great?

# A Prayer to Pray

*Dear God,*
*I'm glad that when trouble comes*
*I don't have to fear it*
*since you send me your help*
*through the Holy Spirit.*
*Amen.*

# A Sleepy Time Activity

Take turns telling how these people
help us: mail carrier; firefighter;
nurse; pastor; police officer. As
you go to sleep, think of how much
the Holy Spirit can love and help
you! Sleep tight.

# A Different Answer

*Jesus said, "Ask and you will receive." John 16:24*

Sam Springly was on his way to buy Daddy's birthday present. Sam was going to buy Daddy his favorite candy bar. "An ooey-gooey Choco-Crunch is the perfect gift!" Sam said as he walked up to Mr. Morisky's store. But when Sam reached in his pocket for the money, what did he find? A hole! Sam's money had fallen out!

Sam searched the sidewalk and checked under rocks; he looked in the grass and even his socks—but the money was gone. "What're you doing?" asked Jimmy Lopez, riding up on Schnickelfritz. Sam sadly said, "I lost the money for Daddy's candy bar. I don't know what to do."

Jimmy thought for a moment. "My Sunday school teacher says: When you don't know what to do, pray to God and he'll answer you!"

So Sam prayed, "Dear God, I lost my money and can't buy Daddy his gift. Could you send an answer? It would give me such a lift! Amen."

*How many rocks do you see?*

Suddenly, Sam spotted something shiny in the grass. "Maybe it's my money!" he shouted. But when Sam looked closer, it was only a candy bar wrapper. "Awww," said Sam, tossing the wrapper aside.

"Wait!" said Jimmy, "What did that wrapper say?" Sam looked again. "Good for one free Choco-Crunch bar!" shouted Sam. "Thank you, God, for hearing me and saving Dad's birthday! You gave me what I asked for—you just answered in a different way!" laughed Sam.

*What did Sam ask for?*
*How did God answer Sam?*

# A Bible Story to Remember
### Acts 12:5-19

When Peter was in jail, his friends asked God for help. God heard their prayers and helped Peter escape. When we need God's help, all we have to do is ask and God will give us what we need! God may answer in a different way than we think he will, but we can trust that he will answer!

# A Prayer to Pray

*Dear God,*
*I'm so glad*
*you're always there*
*to hear and answer*
*every prayer.*
*Amen.*

# A Sleepy Time Activity

Night-Light wants to draw a picture and you can, too. Draw a picture of something you can ask God for. Then hold your picture as you go to sleep and know that God will answer you in his time and in his way! Good night.

# A New Everything

*Jesus said, "I am making everything new!" Revelation 21:5*

Sam and Sophie Springly watched Daddy paint the spare room with blue paint. Mommy was hanging new curtains in the windows. "Why is Grandpa Springly coming to live with us?" asked Sophie. Mommy explained, "Because he needs a new home, Sophie, and he wants to be near people who love him."

"And because we want to share our family with Grandpa," smiled Daddy. "We can make room for Grandpa in our house and in our hearts! It will be a new family for Grandpa, in a new house with a new room."

"There's a new everything!" said Sam. A new carpet was on the floor and Daddy had hung a new wooden door. There were new pictures on the table by the bed, and a new chair cushion in cherry red.

"I wish I had a new place being fixed up for me!" said Sophie, looking around the room.

*What colors do you see?*

199

"You do!" said Daddy. "Jesus is preparing a new home for all of us in heaven. And someday we can all live with God in his mansion!"

"That's cool!" said Sam excitedly. Sophie sighed, "But I'd still like a new room now." "Well, we can do that!" Mommy laughed. "Run and put on your paint shirts. We'll paint your rooms, too."

"Yay!" shouted Sophie and Sam, getting their paint shirts. Sophie smiled and said, "A new room for Grandpa, a new room for us, and a whole new home in heaven! A new everything!"

*How did the Springly's prepare Grandpa's new room?*
*Point to the paintbrushes.*

# A Bible Story to Remember

### Revelation 21:1–22:5

Grandpa has a new room, and we can have a new home in heaven! Jesus is in heaven preparing a place for us to live with God because he wants to be with us forever. We'll live in a beautiful new home filled with love, a new home in heaven with our Father above.

# A Prayer to Pray

*Dear God,*
*Thank you for making*
*everything new*
*and for promising that*
*I can live with you!*
*Amen.*

# A Sleepy Time Activity

Would you like to play a game with Night-Light? Take turns telling about your room in heaven and what you'd like to have new in it. Then as you go to sleep, thank Jesus for making a special home filled with love just for us. Night-night!

God bless you and good night!

# Scripture Index

## "God said" verses

## *"Jesus said" verses*

**Susan L. Lingo** has spent most of her life working with and writing for children of all ages. A former early childhood and elementary school teacher, Susan is the author of over fifty-five Christian books and resources for kids, teachers, and parents—including the bestselling Gold Medallion nominee, *My Good Night® Bible.* Susan's lively approach and age-appropriate style come together again in *My Good Night® Storybook* to create a unique children's devotional storybook that communicates God's Word in a way that preschoolers can relate to, enjoy, and remember. Using soothing rhythm and rhyme, Susan hopes to help busy parents and children share a peaceful, cozy time and learn about God's love and wisdom together. Susan and her husband reside in Loveland, Colorado, with their two children, Lindsay and Dane. When she's not busy creating great projects as the owner and operator of Bright Ideas Books and Book Production, Susan enjoys her cats, tennis, golf, reading, and of course, working with children.

**Kathy Parks** first began drawing around age three, using leftover paper from her uncle's print shop. She has been a fashion illustrator, courtroom artist, commercial artist, and the illustrator of over 200 music lesson books. She has illustrated several other books for Standard Publishing, including *My Good Night® Bible.* In *My Good Night® Storybook*, her delightful designs express the freedom found within the protective structure of God's grace. Her adorable characters were inspired by a lifetime of loving friends, family, and students. Kathy teaches Sunday school in San Diego, California, where she lives with her husband and their two children.

# MY GOOD NIGHT Snuggle-up FAVORITES

### *My Good Night® Bible* (03623)

Forty-five Old and New Testament Bible stories will capture the heart and imagination of your preschooler, and become a favorite part of your bedtime routine. *My Good Night® Bible* was an ECPA Gold Medallion Award finalist.

### *My Good Night® Prayers* (04026)

This companion book features forty-five topical quiet times that follow the themes and scriptures in *My Good Night® Bible* and *My Good Night® Storybook*.

### *Glow & Sing Night-Light Plush* (02910)

This lovable firefly character comes to life as a light-up plush! Squeeze him and he lights up. Then Night-Light sings his special slumber song and wishes kids "Good night, sleep tight!"

### *My Good Night® Bible Songs* (04008)

Your child will love to play songs like "Jesus Loves Me," "Zacchaeus," and "Hallelu, Hallelu" on easy-to-follow color-coded keys. Night-Light shares a thought about each Bible story, too.